6. 50
a

9-28-71

Medieval Skepticism and Chaucer

Medieval Skepticism
and Chaucer

AN EVALUATION OF THE SKEPTICISM OF THE 13TH
AND 14TH CENTURIES OF GEOFFREY CHAUCER AND HIS
IMMEDIATE PREDECESSORS—AN ERA THAT LOOKED BACK
ON AN AGE OF FAITH AND FORWARD TO AN AGE OF REASON

by

MARY EDITH THOMAS, Ph.D.

COOPER SQUARE PUBLISHERS, INC.
NEW YORK
1971

Originally Published 1950 by The William-Frederick Press
Copyright © 1950 by Mary Edith Thomas
Reprinted by Permission of The William-Frederick Press
Published 1971 by Cooper Square Publishers, Inc.
59 Fourth Avenue, New York, N. Y. 10003
International Standard Book No. 0-8154-0379-8
Library of Congress Catalog Card No. 73-147314

Printed in the United States of America

1619940

To

MY MOTHER

Contents

Acknowledgments

WHATEVER VALUE THIS WORK MAY HAVE IS DUE LARGELY TO the interest and help of Professor Roger S. Loomis, of Columbia University. His own high standards of scholarship have, I know, given me a sense of values which not only made this a better work than it could have been without his guidance but which will influence any future work I may do. There is no way to express adequately my appreciation of his help, his many painstaking readings of the manuscript, his encouragement when, the "lyf so short, the craft so long to lerne," I was not certain whether I should "flete or synke."

To Professor Adriaan J. Barnouw, Professor Ernest A. Moody, and Professor Donald L. Clark, all of Columbia University, I wish to express my gratitude for scholarly opinion on the subject and for suggestions about style. Professor Austin Evans, also of Columbia, was good enough to correct certain historical errors.

Dean Richard McKeon of the University of Chicago and Professor E. P. Kuhl of the State University of Iowa, who were generous enough to read the manuscript, made a number of comments that were helpful.

As is self-evident in the text, I have consulted many works of the late Professor G. G. Coulton, whose volumes on subjects related to medieval skepticism have been valuable. I must add that the references he sent to me a few years ago—when, during the war, his notes were not available and he kindly reached back into his rich memory for material—were of considerable help in my early research.

For their advice in the work of translation I am particularly indebted to Dr. Edith F. Claflin, of Columbia University; Dr. Josephine Vallerie, of the College of New Rochelle; and Miss Marion Hendrickson, of Spence School, New York City.

[1]

It would not be possible to name all the people at Columbia University who by their help have made my work easier and by their friendship have made it a happy and stimulating experience. A few, however, it gives me pleasure to mention. Miss Jacqueline Castles, of Carpenter Library, always helpful and considerate, gave most generously of her time, making accessible to me materials that it would have been otherwise difficult for me to secure. Mrs. Adele Mendelsohn and Miss Margaret Bohan, of the staff of the Department of English, have also done many favors, and with a cheerfulness that I shall remember gratefully.

To the late William Volker, Kansas City, Missouri, whose benefactions not only facilitated all my years of college but made possible the publication of this volume, and to his assistant, Miss Juanita Forgey, whose constant advice and guidance helped solve many problems, I owe whatever progress I have made in my studies.

I can acknowledge only generally the help and encouragement of many friends and members of my family—especially my mother, Mrs. Susan M. Thomas, and my husband, Joel S. Branham, to name but two—who have spent countless hours checking manuscripts, searching for books, and relieving me of tedious tasks that are involved in a work of this kind.

Scholarship is what Professor Marjorie H. Nicolson calls a cooperative affair, and I am deeply appreciative of the combined efforts which this volume represents.

M. E. T.

IOWA CITY, IOWA
March 31, 1950

Preface

THE GENERAL CONCEPTION OF THE MIDDLE AGES AS AN AGE
of faith is, in the main, correct. However notorious the iniqui-
ties of the clergy, whatever the failings of the Church, that
institution was the greatest force for good in the life of a people
for whom existence was often full of hardship, and they yielded
their minds to its guidance. Even G. G. Coulton, who, in describing the decay of the monastic orders, has so often painted
the dark side of medieval life, looked upon the Church of the
Middle Ages as the chief civilizing influence of the time. "For
on the whole, when all is told, the human mind deals with
spiritual as with bodily food; there is a slow but steady assimi-
lation of the good, with a corresponding elimination of the
evil; and the spiritual food of the Middle Ages contained (it
is generally admitted) much of the best that has ever been
thought and written by man."[1] The vast majority looked to the
Church for this spiritual food and accepted it unquestioningly.

Nevertheless, there was always a minority, from doubting
Thomas to the humanists of the Renaissance, who found it
difficult to take the mysteries of the Christian religion on faith,
and some who went to the extremes of infidelity. M. Gilson has
remarked:

It is often said, and not without good reasons, that the civilization of the Middle Ages was an essentially religious one. Yet
even in the times of the Cathedrals and of the Crusades, not
everybody was a saint; it would not even be correct to suppose
that everybody was orthodox, and there are safe indications that
confirmed unbelievers could be met on the streets of Paris and
of Padua around the end of the thirteenth century.[2]

That heresies of one sort or another sprang up during the
Age of Faith is of course known to everyone—heresies which

challenged the official interpretation of dogma and denied the authority of the papacy, but did not question the basic tenets of the Christian religion: the existence, the justice, and the omnipotence of God, the fall and the redemption of man, the future life of rewards and punishments. Those who held such independent views we may call heretics but not skeptics. Furthermore, every student of the period knows that there was widespread and vigorous criticism of the clergy, and that the most devout were often the most fiery in their denunciation. But again, though these critics objected to the conduct of the Church's ministers, they did not question their divine sanction. Such protests represent anticlericalism, not skepticism. They struck at the branches, not at the trunk or the roots of the Catholic Church.

But doubt and denial of a more fundamental kind existed, though we learn of the facts largely from those who confessed their past temptations and errors or from those stout champions of orthodoxy who condemned these lapses from faith. Outspoken rejection of cardinal beliefs is naturally rare. As Professor Sarton asserts, it was unsafe not to comply with the authorities, though "outward conformity was offset by considerable individualism, open or secret," and by signs of "imprudent criticism, skepticism, and even (very rarely) of agnosticism."[3] Coulton agrees that "Free thought was driven underground . . . yet it could not be altogether exorcised."[4]

In the pages which follow we shall be concerned with the evidences of skepticism in its various manifestations, except that we shall not attempt to deal with the subtler speculations of the followers of Averroes. The rare atmosphere of metaphysics is not for us. Though reference will be made to the daring questions debated in the schools and to the supposed influence of Averroes on popular thinking, we shall confine ourselves to the problems as they presented themselves to men and women of simpler understanding or those who, like Dante, wrote for a wide public. We shall use the word skepticism, in default of any better single term, to cover a number of mental attitudes. There was troubled *perplexity* as to the how or the why of some basic tenet of Christianity—an attitude which was by no means incompatible with stout adherence to that doctrine, and which many faithful sons and daughters of the Church were obliged to take. There was also *criticism,* a dissatisfaction with the official explanations or formulations of dogma. There was *agnosticism,* a conviction that, while a cardinal doctrine might or might not be true, there was no convincing evidence for it; and this of course was heresy. And there was even worse heresy, a downright *disbelief,* a denial of the teachings of the Church as irrational or improbable. Taken in this wide sense, skepticism may have tinged the thought of a very considerable minority in the later Middle Ages, but the agnostics and infidels must always have been comparatively few, in spite of the sweeping generalizations of satirists or preachers.

The scope of this inquiry will be limited to the thirteenth and fourteenth centuries, not because evidence of skepticism is lacking from earlier and later periods, but because we are particularly concerned with the impact of such thinking on the writings of Chaucer. The world of ideas in which the poet lived was predominantly, of course, that of his own and the preceding age; and it is of interest to observe how some of the recurrent questionings and protests of those periods are echoed in his lines. That he can be classed as anticlerical is hardly to be doubted in view of the fact that four of the five churchmen sketched in the Prologue of the *Canterbury Tales* (the Monk, the Prioress, the Friar, the Pardoner) were in greater or less degree false to their profession. Only the Parson is an ideal figure, and he, as Professor Loomis has shown, would have been recognized by any contemporary reader as a Lollard. But besides satirizing the clergy, like his orthodox contemporaries, Langland and Gower, Chaucer gives expression in various passages to uncertainties and doubts which if they had been carried to the extreme of denial would place him among the infidels. In the prologue to the *Legend of Good Women* he asks whether there is a heaven or a hell, and goes so far as to say that we must take their existence purely on faith. In the

[5]

Knight's Tale Palamon voices with great eloquence and feeling a rebuke to the cruel gods who govern man's lot, award suffering to the innocent, prosperity to the guilty, and eternal torment in the hereafter. Though the ideas are largely borrowed from Boethius, Chaucer does not, like Boethius, answer these criticisms of the divine justice. In the legend of Philomela and in the tales of the Clerk and the Franklin there are poignant questions as to why God should allow evil, physical or moral, to bring undeserved suffering. It is noteworthy that in every instance Chaucer did not find the ideas in the sources of these narratives; it was the poet himself who injected the issues, and who failed to give a direct answer. It will be one of the main purposes of this study to weigh the significance of these and other passages in relation to the rest of his work and in relation to the skeptical tendencies of his time. Then, perhaps, we shall be in a position to tell how far these questionings represent his mature convictions.

It is not, we trust, anticipating too much the results of the investigation to propose that in the raising of these problems of immortality, of divine providence, of the existence of evil, Chaucer was echoing some of the questions which disturbed the minds of his contemporaries, as they have disturbed the thoughtful in other times and places. If "Chaucer was not fertile in original thinking," as the late J. S. P. Tatlock said in reference to the question of Chaucer's orthodoxy, then what he wrote must have been inspired by others, and not merely by his favorite authors. Lowes has rightly called attention to the fact that Chaucer was not merely a poet's poet, but a man among men.

. . . Sources other than the *books* Chaucer read—sources that lie in his intercourse with men and in his reaction upon the interests, the happenings, the familiar matter of his day—entered likewise into "that large compass of his," and must be taken into account in estimating his work.[5]

If this be true, then it is clear that we must know what questions were in the air, what doubts were being voiced when

[6]

Chaucer wrote. A survey of medieval skepticism is a necessary preliminary to the understanding of one phase of his thought.

Naturally this book is greatly indebted to those scholars who have treated the intellectual life of the Middle Ages, particularly in its less orthodox phases. Coulton dealt with it in *Five Centuries of Religion* and *From St. Francis to Dante,* but he was chiefly concerned with the corruption of the clergy and the decay of the religious orders. Adam Storey Farrar in *A Critical History of Free Thought* and John M. Robertson in *A Short History of Free Thought* traced the rise of Protestantism and the effect of Greek and Roman philosophy on Christian thought, commenting on the resistance of the human mind to Christianity, manifested in two ways: skepticism and unbelief. Etienne Gilson dealt with various aspects of skepticism in his discussion of philosophical and theological literature in *Reason and Revelation in the Middle Ages.* J. A. MacCulloch devoted a chapter of his *Medieval Faith and Fable* to the skeptics, emphasizing the significance of thirteenth-century materialism, which provoked questioning about Christian doctrine. W. E. H. Lecky's *Rationalism in Europe* and Henri Busson's *Les Sources et le développement du rationalisme dans la littérature française de la Renaissance* are histories of intellectual growth through the ages and the religious conflicts that resulted particularly from the impact of ancient philosophy on early writers. Skeptical tendencies among the learned are discussed by Pierre Mandonnet in his *Siger de Brabant et l' averroïsme latin au XIIIme siècle,* with particular reference to Arab philosophy. This is likewise the subject of Ernest Renan's *Averroës et averroïsme,* which Coulton described as a valuable work that touched only the fringe of medieval skepticism, a subject deserving a volume to itself. The rebellion against tradition and authority, as opposed to reason, culminating in widespread questioning among medieval people, was the thesis of Mary Morton Wood in *The Spirit of Protest in Old French Literature.* Greta Hort also considered the questioning spirit of the time that led to open protest and heresy, in *Piers Plowman and Contemporary Religious Thought.* All these works, ad-

[7]

mirable as they are, either treat the thirteenth and fourteenth centuries incidentally, or direct the whole attention to the philosophers rather than the literary men, or are chiefly concerned with a single country or writer; Chaucer is referred to briefly, when at all.

Other scholars have, however, written about Chaucer and speculated upon his beliefs. Looten, in *Chaucer, ses modèles, ses sources, sa religion,* discussed Chaucer as a religious man, with particular reference to his anticlericalism. Lounsbury in *Studies in Chaucer* did deal at some length with the signs of agnosticism or infidelity in the poet's work and argued that these represented the settled convictions of his maturity. But Lounsbury's interpretation of the evidence has not met with acceptance and needs to be critically examined.

The treatment in the following pages of so large and so delicate a subject as the spirit of doubt and negation in the Age of Faith and its possible influence on one of the greatest poets of that age will have its shortcomings, and readers may find cause for disagreement. Yet no one will deny that the matter is of importance to intellectual and literary history. The materials are here assembled in greater completeness than has hitherto been achieved; and each reader is free to form his own opinion as to their significance.

1.   The Thirteenth Century

Once, some force created a world, set it spinning in space, and for eons it has pursued its ordered if tempestuous way. Since the moment when one of its living organisms—called man, after millions of years of evolution—scrambled awkwardly from all fours, stood upright on his own feet, and began to contemplate his world and to think about it, he has been perplexedly and perpetually trying to explain the everlasting evils he found cropping up around him.

The evils of the world, proceeding either from the operation of natural laws or from social conflict, have provoked prodigious groans that echo noisily down the centuries. And above the groans rise voices of conjecture, reason, or faith, which ultimately pose the perennial and wistful question, "What can a man believe?" Many moderns are prone to look back on the good old days of calm acquiescence and belief and to long for the easy serenity of the medieval Age of Faith. But they need only look below the surface—and often not too deeply—to find the same unrest, the same doubts and fears, the same insoluble questions that have troubled the minds of men from time immemorial, in the Middle Ages as in the twentieth century.

Today's sophisticate may, with some scorn or pity, look down his nose at the Middle Ages as a period of gross ignorance, superstition, and quiet acceptance. True, we can see in the life of the time a lack of knowledge and a dependence upon unreliable authority, but if medieval men did not have available so complete a mass of technical and scientific facts as we, they were quite able to construct a theological system that dealt with man's place in the universe. It was a brilliant and acute mind that exercised itself in ordering the hierarchy of angels. Whether the medieval mind was right or wrong is not our concern; what is important is that it achieved a well ordered system of thought and a cosmic viewpoint.

If we find a fundamentally religious tone in many written records of the Middle Ages it is because serious literature was long dominated by the Church, which controlled the editing and production of books; much of what was written down shows the strong influence of ecclesiastical authority. The danger of discussing ideas incompatible with Church doctrine limited the open expression of infidelity; much "still went on under the surface, yet no medieval thinker could openly transgress the main conventional limits, unless here and there some fortunate accident might protect him."[1] Such thoughts as were censored persisted, all the same, until a few of the bolder thinkers dared put pen to parchment. By the thirteenth century, the prevalence of infidelity, according to Coulton, "may be established by details as manifold and as startling as those which I have briefly summarized [*From St. Francis to Dante*] to indicate the prevailing ignorance and irreverence."[2] And by the fourteenth century a number of outspoken writers had begun to reflect a trend of thought which was tinged with skepticism and which betrayed individual opinion and freedom from tradition.

While the skeptics of the thirteenth century did not often give written expression to unorthodox thinking, in the works of religious men directed against such doubters we have a marked indication of skepticism among at least a few. Very early in the century Guiot de Provins wrote a long poem, *La Bible* (1204-1209), to reproach the clergy for the widespread unbelief that he had observed among the people. He claimed that he only mirrored the world and wrote without anger or resentment. The poet's purpose seems to have been to amuse as much as to edify, though he was often sharply critical:

> In faith, the secular clergy
> I see badly deceived:
> They make the world disbelieve.
> The clerks and priests act in such a way,

So do the secular canons,
If they make people despair.[3]

He denounced the immorality of the clergy and reproved them as well for their unfaith:

But I see them so lost
In sin and in covetousness
That they have brought despair
To the people, who very soon disbelieve.
They themselves, I think, disbelieve.[4]

The devout, and warmly human, Berthold of Regensburg (*fl.* 1250), one of the greatest of the medieval preachers, also left an eloquent record in which we can discern something of what went on in the minds of the people. In his sermons we find him frequently stopping to answer dissenting voices from his congregation; clearly his people were troubled about matters of faith. Always colorful, often poetic, Berthold used simple metaphors to stimulate imagination and quicken religious fervor:

The third thing that arouses unbelief is symbolized by the moon. See now, how many thousands of men therewith become lost, so that they never see the high and true sun! . . . Now have pity yourselves, that God may have pity on you, because many a man is damned for unbelief. Thus, the moon symbolizes unbelief, because unbelief is of so many kinds. The heathen have so many and such various kinds of unbelief that no one can name them all. . . . And thereby the moon symbolizes unbelief, for the moon, thoroughly inconstant, goes through so many phases. Today she is young, tomorrow old; today she wanes, tomorrow waxes; now small, now large; now she goes high in the heaven, tomorrow she goes low; now here, now there; now this, now that. Just so are unbelieving people.[5]

The writers of the time attributed such unbelief to a variety of causes. Gautier de Coincy (1177-1236) blamed ignorance, stubborn will, and boldness. In his collection *Les Miracles de la Sainte Vierge*, Gautier's satire against all unbelievers, scattered incongruously through the pages of the charming narratives,

[11]

reveals a poet who is also an earnest and austere moralist. He berated those who no longer cared to hear about the miracles of the Virgin, those who called them false.

In the thirteenth century when she dominated the imaginations of men, criticism of the Virgin Mary is significant of the loss of faith that people had suffered. The cult of the Virgin was a favorite theme of poets. To the faithful, God represented justice but the Virgin embodied the more human quality of mercy. She interceded for men as their spiritual mediator, rewarded yearnings for tenderness and kindness; she blessed the humble of spirit, soothed the troubled of mind and heart. Devotion to Mary is variously demonstrated: in religious lyrics, the Ave Marias, hymns "To Our Lady," supplications for mercy; and pictorially in art, especially the stained glass of the cathedrals—like the glorious window of Chartres dedicated to the "Queen of Heaven." Henry Adams has shown how poignantly this devotion was manifested among medieval men and women: "How passionately they worshipped Mary, the Cathedral of Chartres shows . . . but still one cannot realize how actual Mary was, to the men and women of the Middle Ages, and how she was present, as a matter of course, whether by way of miracle or as a habit of life, throughout their daily existence."[6]

In view of the ardent personal feeling for Mary, it is surprising that even she did not escape criticism.

> Indeed he who does not honor her,
> And truly believe in her miracles,
> Does not believe God exists
> Or that God has any power.[7]

Gautier's denunciation of those who doubted the miracles of the Virgin implies a considerable number of faithless folk.[8]

For the peasants, whom he found most stubbornly irreligious, Gautier reserved his harshest invectives:

> The peasants are so foolish and bold
> That they are as brutish as beasts;
> They will not observe the saints' days,

Or do anything the priest says. . . .
Toward God they are so callous
That they are harder than this wall.
They do not fear God any more than they do a sheep,
And would not give a button
For the sacred commands of Holy Church. . . .
They have little belief and little faith.[9]

To this default of faith Gautier attributed their poverty, their afflictions, their misery. But the upper class, the learned, by no means escaped his notice:

Even among the lettered I know some
Who by venom are so poisoned
That their hearts do not delight at all
In the grace of the Holy Spirit. . . .
They often make simple folk doubt,
Because they jest and laugh
At some of the things the folk say.[10]

According to Gautier, people did not value the miracles . . . they lacked belief and faith . . . they did not believe holy Scripture . . . they doubted that God could have been born of a virgin.[11] Where is the obedience to the teaching of the preachers, the religious unity as conceived by the modern looking back on the Middle Ages through an aura of sentiment and longing? Coulton has rightly suggested that "The uniformity of medieval faith has often been much exaggerated by modern writers: thoughtful and plain-spoken writers of the time often show indications of embarrassment."[12] Certainly the people whom Gautier described were not conspicuously devout!

Etienne de Bourbon (*fl.* 1261) blamed, not ignorance and boldness, but the Devil for the spread of such unbelief:

The devil tempts people profoundly and secretly, either subtly in the matter of faith or with a spirit of blasphemy, by which, when other means fail him, he frequently tempts pious and especially simple souls, in order to lead them into despair or keep them from the good. I have seen a pious and religious and upright clerk tested in his novitiate by the temptation (of

[13]

doubt), first as to whether the world were anything but a dream, whether he himself had a soul, and even whether there were a God.[13]

By the number and vehemence of their protests, these men of religion unwittingly attest the prevalence of skepticism in the Age of Faith. Even if we discount the zealot's exaggeration and the rhetorician's eloquence, we must reckon with the bulk of their accusations against unbelievers.

Members of the Orders were not left untouched by agonies of doubt, torn as they often were between the questioning of their minds and the most devout desires of their hearts, as Caesarius of Heisterbach testifies:

A certain nun, very elderly and, it was supposed, of great holiness, was so disturbed by the vice of melancholy, distressed to such a degree by the spirit of blasphemy, doubt, and distrust, that she fell into despair. Those things which from infancy she had believed and was bound to believe, she began to doubt completely, nor could she be induced by anyone to take part in the holy sacrament. When the sisters, even her own granddaughter, asked why she was thus hardened, she answered: "I am among the reprobates, that is, one of those who are to be damned." One day the Prior, much disturbed, said to her: "Sister, unless you recover from this belief, when you die I shall have you buried in unconsecrated ground."[14]

This good woman was driven to such lengths by her despair that she threw herself into the Moselle river. Here is no steady, sustaining assurance of one who lived in the Age of Faith! It is downright infidelity in its most desolating form.

The thirteenth century was a century of disputation. Many intellectuals of the time poured considerable energy into long argumentative tracts, treatises, books, which discussed theological and philosophical problems.[15] Somehow their current of thought reached the layman and the unschooled, who, too, became interested. Note the unusual popularity of a book which probably derived from an oriental prototype, *The Book of Sidrach*. The French redactor was a man without culture, who wrote badly and with no sense of style, and obviously addressed himself to the unlettered. Langlois described him as "épicurien, égoïste, cynique, grossier."[16] The identity of this "Pseudo-Sidrach" remains unknown but he was almost certainly a clerk of the western world, perhaps a Provençal, who had access to a library of ecclesiastical works in Latin. The work has not been dated with any certainty; the author claimed to be writing in 1243, but Langlois inclines to believe it a later work, composed probably between 1268 and 1291. The popularity of the book was enormous; it is found listed in all the royal libraries of the fourteenth and fifteenth centuries, and was translated during the Middle Ages into Italian, Flemish, Middle Low German, English, Hebrew, and Latin. Langlois says it was one of the books of the Middle Ages which had the greatest popularity up to the Renaissance.

Sidrach,[17] typical of a sort of book in vogue during the Middle Ages, presents a simple exposition of Christian doctrine by the method of catechism. The author prefaces his work with a long series of leading questions: Why did not God make man incapable of sin? Why did He make the world? Why did He lay man open to a short, disordered life, to poverty, to weakness, etc.; why did He not assure man of paradise? Why does man suffer in this world? Is God responsible for the good and evil done on earth? Is one to blame God for the misfortunes that happen? Must one believe the philosophers who say that there is no other world than this?[18] These were the things people were talking about, the questions they were asking. Sidrach was far from successful in submitting satisfying answers and, like many other men of his time, had to take refuge in the unfathomable mystery of the divine will, reproving those who questioned the acts of God. "He who sets out to know thoroughly about the power of God is as foolish as the one who would like to enclose the brightness of the sunshine in his house."[19]

As the minds of the people became confused by these issues and by theological disputes about the existence and wisdom of God, the tenets of the Church were called into question; immortality was among the first to be examined. A work in Pro-

vençal known as *Las Novas del heretje* appeared about 1242.
In this piece the inquisitor Izarn makes accusations against a
heretic, Sicart de Figueiras, whose recantation is believed by
some scholars to have historical basis. Among other charges,
Izarn accuses Sicart of denying immortality: "Thou hast
denied and abandoned thy faith and thy baptism. . . . Thou
dost not believe that [the soul of] man or woman can rise
again."[20]

Robert de l'Omme, who probably lived in the small town
of Lomme in northern France, was likewise concerned about
the general lack of regard for Christian worship and the indifference of people to the welfare of their souls. In *Le Miroir de
vie et de mort* (1266) Robert, admonishing the world to think
more seriously about the future life, was troubled by the
materialists, those who in time of death gave more attention to
an expensive tomb for the deceased than to prayers for his
soul.

When he dies, they make a slab [tomb] for him
As if his soul were still in there.
Every man and woman, astonished at it,
Says: "It is well made."
Then they go directly away from there;
They do not say another prayer for his soul.
Many people think of the soul
That it is nothing but wind.[21]

Heaven and hell were vivid realities to the medieval people,
and doubts concerning the hereafter indicate a critical attitude
toward a matter that was vital to them.

In a world in which existence was hard, and the only refuge
for the multitude lay in the hope of a future life, their readiness to question immortality signifies an important spiritual
loss in their lives. This loss produced, among some of the folk
incapable of abstract thinking, a kind of fatalism and resignation. Caesarius finds them refusing conversion because, they
say, "When the day of my death comes, I shall die; I shall
not be able to put it off by living well, nor anticipate it by
living badly."[22]

[16]

A large body of vision literature indicates to what an extent the imagination was concerned with the spirit world, and contemporary records report many supernatural experiences. Trances, miracles, visitations, these were alternately accepted as manifestations of God and works of the Devil. The difficulty in distinguishing one from the other, the evil spirit from the good, provoked alarm and doubt. Did spirits come from heaven or hell? or did they appear at all? There was "a serious desire to ridicule the belief to which the visions testified—an example of medieval scepticism."[23] Coulton writes: "Men's faith was perplexed on all sides by visions and miracles often proved to be false. . . . The greatest saints had often the bitterest struggles: first with their own family and the World: then with religious doubts."[24]

When there was actual rejection of visions, the medieval preacher blamed materialistic forces which persuaded men to hold suspect what they could not themselves prove. Caesarius relates this story, told him by an abbot of Brumbach: A girl of wealth and of great beauty went into the Church against the wishes of her parents. But after she had taken her vows, her faith began to waver and she soon fell into despair. When the abbot, to whose care she had been entrusted, came to her, the troubled girl poured out her heart to him:

"Ill I live, ill I fare, and I do not know at all why or on whose account I am secluded here. . . . Who knows if there be a God, if there be angels with Him, souls, or a kingdom of heaven? Who has seen these things? who on returning from that place has shown us what he saw? . . . I speak according to the way it seems to me. Unless I should see these things, I will not believe."[25]

Peter, Prior of Holy Trinity, Aldgate, London (1197-1221), likewise deplored the challenge of common sense that roused serious doubts of the unseen. He pointed out that, though nearly all nations of mankind had cast away their idols and believed in one God, yet there were still some who believed that there was no God at all and that the world was ruled by

[17]

chance; that there were many who considered "only what they see, believing neither in good nor in evil angels, nor in life after death, nor in any other spiritual and invisible things."[26]

As an example of spiritual struggle, the tendency to waver between faith and doubt, Peter tells the story of a mourning father, crushed by the most universal of all experiences, and one which most often tries even the profoundest faith in another world—death.

After the death of this child, the holy man [Ailsi] began to ponder within himself concerning the future state of the blest; but, seeing that neither he, as a layman, knew aught thereof, nor could any other man give him any sure tidings, he remained in great anxiety of mind.[27]

But Ailsi was a "holy man," as most of the people were not, and the pathos of involuntary unbelief is lacking in the popular expression of the man in the street. Thomas of Cantimpré (1200-1270) tells how men, drinking at the inn and engaging in small talk of the time, would speak of what shall be after this life. They would say, "We are utterly deceived by those clerks, who say that our souls outlive the destruction of the body!" and then all would fall a-laughing.[28] These were the kind of men who already in the thirteenth century were anticipating the doubts of FitzGerald's *Rubaiyat* and were willing to "take the Cash and let the Credit go." Not having found any providence but fate, and any world but the present, they were ready to make the most of it.

The devout Monk of Froidmont describes as "fools" these irresponsible scoffers who jest about serious matters:

> [They say]   "What does it matter to us
> At what hour death assails us?
> Let us take now the good which comes to us!
> Afterwards, let come what may:
> Death is the end of the fight
> And the soul and body are destroyed."[29]

[18]

Rutebeuf (*fl.* 1250-85) denounces with similar indignation the one who takes life too lightly, who

         . . . believes nothing,
Does not think that there is a hell or heaven,
Or that he has a soul and body because he does not perceive it;
Rather does the profound one think that sin deceives him.
"How," says the unbeliever, "can it be true,
What the clerks tell us in their theology:
When the soul is freed and comes before God,
They say that it is more beautiful than the body was."
"I could not believe," says the complete heretic,
"What Scripture says nor what the clergy teaches." . . .
Such people are very clearly unbelievers:
They say that the soul does not separate from the body or
     change. . . .
Now there are other heretics so unbelieving in God
That they do not believe God is so powerful,
When the dead body has decayed, that in the same form
God can remake it as it was before.[30]

The churchmen, Giraldus Cambrensis, Caesarius, Peter the Prior, Matthew Paris, Etienne, Berthold, speak of the agonies of genuinely devout minds. Giraldus (*c.* 1146-1220), in the course of his turbulent career, learned much about the social and intellectual life of his day. He may have been filled with vanity, prejudice, intense patriotism, and violent party spirit, but his power of observation makes him a valuable witness to conditions as he found them. Giraldus the pessimist, troubled about the spread of infidelity, deplored the unbelief among the clergy, of whom he told many stories:

A certain priest in our times, flaming with the zeal of charity and reform, had privately rebuked for many faults another priest who he knew celebrated the divine rites and consecrated the body of the Lord with little devotion and reverence. At last he rebuked him chiefly for this: that he performed the sacrament of the body and blood of God dishonorably, and because he used wafers neither as pure and white as was fitting, nor even fresh and suitable, but old and broken, for the sacrifice. The accused man answered him in this way: "What is it that you are saying?

[19]

You deserve odium with your religion. Do you suppose flesh is made from this bread and blood from this wine? Nay, do you suppose that God, the Creator of all things, assumed flesh from a woman? That he wanted to suffer? Do you suppose a woman conceived without union or remained a virgin after giving birth? Also, do you suppose our bodies, once having been reduced to dust, will rise again? All the things we do are hypocrisy." . . . O, how many like this one lie hidden among us today![31]

Here was a thoroughgoing rationalist who had applied to Scripture such a rigid test of common sense as we should, rather, expect of the twentieth-century skeptic; and, while holding onto outer observances, had completely repudiated the doctrines which underlay them.

Even the Pope, Boniface VIII (1228-1303), charged with many infamies, was accused of denying the dogmas. Boniface made no pretensions to spiritual perfection and never tried to hide his ambition and avarice. His open quarrel with Philip the Fair of France, himself as ambitious and avaricious as his papal antagonist, is worthy of note for the reckless and arrogant tone in the accusations Philip brought against a person in a position of such sacred trust. Philip had the audacity to address one of his communications flippantly: "Philip, by the grace of God king of the French, to Boniface, who claims to be the Pope; little greeting, or rather none at all."[32] Boniface had been attacked not only for simony and immorality but for outright infidelity. His critics specifically charged him with having denied immortality; and he was directly quoted thus, in one instance:

"You fools sillily believe a foolish thing! Who ever came back from the other world, to tell us anything about it? Happy they who know how to enjoy life; and pitiable creatures are those who lose the present life in hopes of gaining a future one, like the dog that stands over a pool of water with a bit of meat in his mouth, and seeing the reflected image of it, lets go the substance to chase after the shadow."[33]

Though the charge that Boniface actually used such language

is not sustained by a particle of evidence,[34] it is a remarkable indication of the times that such a story could circulate about the Pope himself.

It is a common enough occurrence to find medieval men of religion criticizing the skeptical thought that was abroad and threatening the religious unity of all classes everywhere. But occasionally criticism is found also among laymen. A soldier, writer, and scholar, born in Lombardy and famed for his skill as a pleader in the courts, spent his old age repenting the follies of his youth and pleading not for legal justice but religious faith. Philippe of Novara (1190?-1264?) in his *Quatre Ages de l'homme* looked back on some seventy years of life and set down his philosophical and moral observations with the authority of a man of the world who had seen much. He drew on his broad studies and varied experience to bring to his readers a better way of life. He made sweeping accusations against those who in ignorance disregarded the teaching of the Church. He reiterated throughout his didactic treatise an assertion that there were many who said there was no other world than this.[35] "So they say, and there are other unbelievers who say, that this world has always been and is and will be, and that no other ever was, nor is, nor ever shall be."[36]

A generation later another soldier and scholar, a man of years, knowledge, and experience, likewise wrote of his youth. Jean de Joinville (1224-1319), like Philippe aged and of devout religious conviction, in his *Histoire de Saint Louis* confessed his own temptations to infidelity. He told how his king, in a crisis, helped strengthen his faith:

The holy King tried his best, by his words, to make me believe strongly in the Christian law that God has given us, just as you shall hear later. He said that we must believe so strongly the articles of the faith that neither death nor any misfortune which might come to the body should give us a desire to go against faith by word or deed. And he said that the Enemy is so subtle that, when people are dying, he works as hard as he can to make them die in some doubt of the articles of the faith.[37]

[21]

Joinville, the historian, did not leave us a comprehensive picture of the times as his predecessor Villehardouin had done, nor a description of the vivid social world, like his successor Frois- sart; but without heroics or boasting he presented an idealized King Louis and, in so doing, a personal record of his own life and mind that was altogether human. He was frank about his own part in affairs of the world. He did not hesitate to show normal fear in battle and concern for his own skin, to reveal a weakness for wine, to confess—when put to it—that he would rather commit thirty mortal sins than be a leper! Grant that Joinville, like Philippe, was aged, and with approaching years had taken on an abnormally pious and severe view of life. Yet his memory seemed clear enough on other matters, and we may take his word for it that the conditions of his age fostered skepticism. He described how the Enemy threatened religion, so subtly attacking the faithful that believers must boldly say: "You will not indeed tempt me not to believe firmly all the articles of the faith."[38]

Joinville had been shocked by the barbarous customs and primitive beliefs of people across the ocean, but he was more distressed by the effect of fatalism upon his own countrymen: "I have seen in this country, since I came back from beyond the sea, several disloyal Christians who held the belief of the Bedouins, and said that no one could die before his day."[39] The author sternly denounced the religious doubt of his con- temporaries, whom he sometimes pictured as men of wavering belief.

Those to whom heaven had become a matter of doubt regarded hell, too, as improbable, even a fabrication to frighten timid souls into obedience. Giraldus quoted such a skeptic as saying, "No doubt men of olden time through caution made up such things in order to strike terror into men and restrain them from rash and daring deeds."[40] Later in the period, the miracle play won great popularity. Though inevitable punish- ment of sin constituted the theme, hell became so commonplace that, filled as it seemed to be with simple folk, it began to appeal as a place where simple folk might well feel at home.

"He who is accustomed to Hell is as comfortable there as else-where," the scandalized Berthold reported that "some folk say," the unabashed skeptic arguing that the soul must eventually, after hundreds of years, become so used to hell that it attained a passive state in which pain could no longer be felt.[41] Medieval folk may have had acquiescent minds and simple souls, for the most part, but they were not sitting about in sackcloth and ashes. And though insensitive to what we smugly call refinements of modern civilization, even they were revolted by the horror of a dogma that consigned the majority of mankind to damnation,[42] and men of religion were everywhere confronted with unanswerable questions about the future life.

If the religious tracts of the period focus upon the somber side of life, often unrelieved by hope of spiritual joy, it need not be supposed that life was devoid of happiness. Medieval people had a rare gift for living with zest and lusty enthusiasm. Their own world might be dark in contrast to the bright other-world of the preachers but it had the advantage of being present.

Nowhere is this lively interest in the here-and-now more apparent than in a thirteenth-century work that is one of the most delightful of all medieval writings, *Aucassin et Nicolette.* It provides one of the rare early examples of skepticism, not as the object of the author's strictures but as the expression of his defiance of ecclesiastical teaching and his revolt against an ascetic morality. In contrast to the typical cleric, the author is mundane and impious. He cannot conceive of a God unsympathetic with the joyous pagan world in which the lovers lived. "God loveth lovers" is a phrase he confidently uses. He boldly secularizes a pious motif when he attributes to Nicolette's physical beauty the miracle of healing a paralytic. But the most notable illustration of the author's unorthodoxy is Aucassin's famous reply to his father's warning that should the youth marry against his parent's wishes he will surely go down to hell:

"In Paradise what have I to gain? I do not seek to enter there, but only to have Nicolette, my sweet lady, that I love so well.

For into Paradise go only such folk as I shall tell you. Thither go these old priests, and lame old men and one-armed ones who all day and all night crouch before the altars and in the old crypts, and such folk as wear old threadbare coats and old tattered frocks, folk who are naked and shoeless and without hose, who are dying of hunger and thirst and of cold and of discomfort; these are the ones who go into Paradise: with them have I nothing to do. But into Hell would I go; for into Hell go the fine clerks and fair knights, who died in tourneys and great wars, and brave men at arms and noble men: with these I prefer to go; and there go the beautiful courtly ladies because they have two lovers, or three, with their husbands; and thither goes the gold, and the silver, and cloth of *vair*, and cloth of *gris*; and thither go harpers, and minstrels, and the princes of the world: with these I would go, if I but have with me Nicolette, my sweetest lady.''[43]

Thus Aucassin voices the thoughts of we know not how many others who would have foregone the forbidding society of the poor old churchmen in heaven for the more gallant company in hell. The speech delights us today by its spirit and youthful exuberance; but in the thirteenth century it must have startled many listeners; for it exalts, as vividly as any other passage in medieval literature, the World and the Flesh and, some would add, the Devil.

If immortality was open to serious doubts, it follows that participation in the Eucharist on which salvation depends would also become a prominent issue. To believers, the liturgy of the Eucharist was—and ever has been—an essential part of Christian worship. When the celebration of Mass fell a prey to criticism and became the object of speculation, it can be understood to what extent the medieval mind was troubled. Rationalists began to apply their own standards to the miracle of transubstantiation. Especially in the universities, where freethinking was most prevalent,[44] were the mysteries subjected to the test of reason. The sacramental bread and wine were no different from any other, according to radical teachers and—subsequently—students.[45] These, however, will be discussed later in connection with skeptical tendencies among the learned.

Churchmen too were not impervious to such freethinking. Salimbene asserted that no less a personage than a bishop of Parma, Gregory the Roman, died a heretic and accursed; for in his last illness, when the sacrament was brought to him he refused to take it and said that he believed nothing of such a faith.[46] And the see of Parma was said to be as safe from undue secular influence as any in Europe.[47]

Joinville told a similar story of a great master of divinity who admitted unbelief to the bishop, William of Paris. Weeping, the holy man had confessed his sin of doubt: "I tell you, Sir, I cannot help weeping; for I believe I am an infidel, because I cannot bring my heart to believe in the sacrament of the altar as Holy Church teaches."[48] The sincerity and anguish of such confessions are apparent.

There was, besides, the perennial problem of God's justice, the inequitable distribution of rewards and punishments on this earth, the prosperity of the wicked and the suffering of the innocent. It was the problem of Job and the problem of Boethius. It was one of the questions which we have seen was raised in *The Book of Sidrach*. Medieval people, repeatedly subjected to the horrors of war, pestilence, and the elements, were sorely perplexed by what seemed the injustices of a cruel God. Too often divine judgment seemed to spring not from a benevolent Father but from a hard master. There must have been some like William Rufus, who, after a serious illness, still refusing to mend his ways, cried out bitterly: "By the Holy Face of Lucca, God shall never have me good for all the evil that He hath brought upon me!"[49]

Pierre Cardinal (*fl.* 1210-30), who sang his verses from court to court, did not always play the part of the lighthearted troubadour but devoted some caustic lines to current issues. He did not accept the God of injustice whom he heard the people talking about; rather, he pledged his faith to a kindly God, but threatened to repudiate Him too should He prove unmerciful:

I shall not despair of you [God]. . . .
If I [should] have evil here, and burn in hell,

> By my faith, it would be wrong and unjust
> So that I could rightly reproach you,
> Since for one good I have a thousand times as much evil.[50]

His tone is singularly irreverent for an age commonly regarded as an age of faith, but Pierre was not struck down for his impiety—and lived to be almost a hundred!

Matheolus (*fl.* 1290), on the other hand, did protest against the ecclesiastical God who arbitrarily dealt out unmerited punishment to all mankind for Adam's sin. Reason told him God must be a power for good; otherwise Christ, who had himself paid for the sins of mankind, would have died in vain. It is the beginning of a rational tolerance not often characterizing medieval thought.

> Ah, God! how well I must complain
> Of thee. . . .
> For, as thou art obliged
> To save all, great and small,
> Why dost thou menace us, sinners,
> And condemn and ensnare us
> Endlessly unto eternal pain
> For a momentary fault? . . .
> Why are we so greatly,
> Eternally tormented
> For a little and slight sin? . . .
> Tell why, by what right,
> For the sin of Adam
> His offspring and his lineage is punished. . . .
> Each must bear his burden
> According to his guilt, small or large. . . .
> It seems to be against justice
> That the lineage be damned
> For a deed of which it is not guilty.[51]

This logical approach to fundamental dogmas and the temerity in calling God to account were unconventional, and the orthodox were shocked into stern refutations.

It was against such rationalism that Philippe of Novara directed his most earnest pronouncements. The will of God was inscrutable and not to be questioned. A medieval Cowper, he saw only that God moves in a mysterious way His wonders to perform, and Philippe never doubted His just purpose. Nor did he try to restrain his impatience with those who complained of God's works.

They are the ones who blaspheme and find fault with the heavenly and earthly works that the Father and Creator made, and say of some things: "This is not well done," and "such and such a thing might be good," and so on. Among other things they say: "Why did God make man to have pain and labor in this world, and tribulations from the time he was born until death? And at the end, if He finds man in any fault, then man goes to hell; yet God surely ought not to have done it." . . . Surely they ought to keep silent who find fault with the works of God. . . . How do they dare say: "Why did God make man?" and "It would be better if he had not done it!"[52]

But even Philippe was hard put to it to explain away the heretical observation that the "good loyal Christians, who do good works and conduct themselves well toward God and the world, often suffer more persecutions and evils in this world than do the evil and unfaithful folk: those in whom are all malice and evils often have many more worldly possessions than the good."[53] It was cold comfort to promise just reward and punishment in another world, which for the realistic of mind and weak of faith never "was, nor is, nor ever shall be."

Joinville heard his pious king also try to explain the ways of God to people who asked this sort of question, who said: "Lord God, why dost thou threaten us? Because in the threats thou makest us, it is not to thy good or thy advantage; for if thou hadst brought us all to ruin [in a storm at sea], thou wouldst, for all that, be no poorer or richer."[54] Louis's explanation that misfortune is sent upon man by God as a gracious warning to purify his soul was not quite convincing to the men who, not unjustifiably, expected at least meager reward in this world for honest effort.

Even an author of chivalric romance, a genre concerned very little with the happenings of everyday life, was not

[27]

unaware of the skeptical trend. Wolfram von Eschenbach, deemed one of the great medieval poets,[55] was a man of wide practical experience and genuine religious fervor. Within the limits of a tale of adventure he had the genius to give his romantic hero Parzival, along with physical strength and all the chivalric virtues, perfectly human qualities. So that even one of Arthur's most perfect knights was allowed to admit a flaw of character: wavering faith and resentment against God's injustice.

In the Fifth Book of Wolfram's *Parzival,* we find the hero at the castle of the Wounded Grail-King. To Parzival is given the chance to deliver the sufferer by asking a question that will lift the curse of affliction which has befallen him. But Parzival, trained for knighthood by Old Gurnemanz, has been warned not to be bold in questioning. Through courtesy, that makes him loath to appear too curious, he fails to put the magic question. Later at Arthur's court his joyful and honored reception is interrupted by the graceless messenger of the Grail, Cundrie, who taunts him for his failure to free the king. Humiliated and disheartened, Parzival makes ready to exile himself from society. He has lost all joy in life, through no deliberate fault of his own, and he will no longer worship a God who rules without justice or mercy.

'Ah, what is God? If He were mighty, if God ruled with power, He would not have put us both to open shame. I served Him loyally and looked for grace. Now I will renounce His service! If He be wroth with me, I will bear it.'[56]

Here Parzival speaks like any high-spirited young man of his time. There is an interval of years, and we see Parzival unburdening to the hermit Trevrizent all the bitterness of his troubled heart and mind:

'Now for the first time do I perceive,' said Parzival, 'how long I have gone unguided, lorn of joy. To me, joy is a dream, grief the burdensome yoke under which I labour.

'Sir, I will tell you more. Wherever, in church or minster, God's praise was sung, no eye has seen me since that day. I have

[28]

cared for naught else but fighting. Yes, and I bear great enmity towards God, for He has fathered my sorrows and made them mighty. My joy is buried alive. If God's power were ready to help, what an anchor my joy would have been! Now it has naught to hold to, grief sucks it down. If my hope is wounded past help, or if it survives the scar wherewith sorrow's sharp crown has branded my knightly prowess, each way I maintain, it is a shame to Him Who has power to help, if all they say of His help be true, that He helps not me!"[57]

Though Wolfram was himself filled with sincere religious fervor, he was "free from the other-worldliness typical of mediaeval Church doctrine."[58] His story is marked by realism, and he catches in his heroes a fundamental quality that is lasting and human. "His poetic vision," Margaret Fitzgerald Richey states in her excellent translation of the work, "expresses a life which he cared for and knew. He not only shows its heroic altitudes: he reveals to us at the same time its familiar levels. . . . He probably did not think differently from the average layman."[59] We have a right to look upon Parzival as a representative man of the thirteenth century. And like other medieval men, his faith shaken by adversity and the apparent wrath of the God he sought to serve, he was, over a period of years, subjected to doubts and questionings.

In the same genre, about the same time, the French author of *La Mort le Roi Artu* voices the same criticism of an unjust God. Like Parzival, Arthur, plunged into despair by his losses at the ill-fated battle of Camelot, finds the divine will less than just. "This loss has come to me not by the justice of God but on account of Lancelot's pride."[60] M. Jean Frappier, editor of the thirteenth-century text, in a reference to this line points out that the conception of God as an angry God contributes heavily to the atmosphere of inevitable destruction which the author creates in the second half of his book. Arthur refuses to recognize divine justice in the misfortunes which befall him at the last battle of Salisbury, and his repeated reproaches to God who has abandoned him "reviennent comme un leitmotiv funèbre":[61] "Ah, God! why do you permit what I see, for the

[29]

world's worst traitor has killed one of the noblest men alive [Yvain, killed by Modred]."[62] And when Modred also kills Sagremor: "Ah, God! why do you allow me to decline so in earthly prowess?"[63] But God remains indifferent to the plea for help, and Arthur's men in turn lament their misfortune, after the duel that proves fatal both to their king and to Modred: "Ah, God, why did you permit this battle?"[64] While this conception of a "Dieu exterminateur" proceeds rather from emotion than from reasoned speculation, M. Frappier notes that "in certain passages it casts a shadow over the religion of the *Mort Artu*."[65]

This theme of troubled dissatisfaction with an unjust God is twice found in one of the earliest collections of exempla—moralistic anecdotes, fables, narratives—known as the *Gesta Romanorum*. For centuries it had the popularity of the romances, and furnished literary materials for writers from the day of Chaucer, Gower, Lydgate, Boccaccio, and Shakespeare up to modern times. Originally intended for the use of preachers as a book of moral edification, the work came by accretion to include the favorite stories of several generations of medieval people.

In his definitive edition of the *Gesta*,[66] Hermann Oesterley describes in detail his examination of 138 medieval manuscripts of the work which appeared in Germany, France, Italy, and England. He divides the manuscripts into three main branches: Latin, German, and English. Between 1472 and 1475 the first edition was printed in Utrecht and reprinted in Cologne, and the Vulgate in Cologne; the first English version was printed by Wynkyn de Worde, 1510-15. Oesterley believes that both the English and Continental manuscripts derive from one group, which was English. First compiled, then, in England, the collection later reached the Continent, where it was modified, enlarged, and corrupted. Oesterley describes the history of the *Gesta* as "one of the most important, but also most obscure and complicated, chapters in the story of world literature."[67] The work is important here for the light it throws upon the old practice of fabricating explanations of things not understood or justifiable by reason, and for its insight into the popular mind.

Although the *Gesta Romanorum* as a collection is now usually dated early in the fourteenth century, probably about 1330, the story that concerns us here, generally known as "The Angel and the Hermit," goes back to the early centuries of the Christian era. The earliest Greek and oriental versions were translated into Latin and appeared in the thirteenth and fourteenth centuries in many languages. Its popularity continued up to the time of Luther, Percy Herbert, Henry More, Parnell, and finally Voltaire. One of the best medieval versions, according to Gaston Paris, belongs to the thirteenth century; "ce conte occupe un des meilleurs rangs dans la poésie narrative du XIII° siècle."[68]

In the various redactions of the story, details may differ, but in general they correspond to the version in the *Gesta*:

A hermit, who lived in a remote cave, one day saw a shepherd tending his flocks. The shepherd fell asleep and a sheep was stolen, whereupon his master had him put to death. Appalled at this injustice, the hermit cried out: "Oh Lord, see how this man placed blame on an innocent person and killed him. Why do you permit such things to happen? I shall go into the world and live as other men do."[69]

Leaving, then, his cave, he set out to become once more a man of the secular world. He lost his way, and an angel appeared before him, a messenger from heaven to guide him. In the course of the next several days the angel killed the baby of a soldier who had given them shelter, stole a gold cup from a citizen who had entertained them, threw into the river a pilgrim of whom they had asked directions, and presented the stolen cup to a man who had refused them the shelter of his home.

The erstwhile hermit was further convinced of God's capricious distribution of good and evil fortune. The angel explains it as a divine plan to prevent sin and to reform character, and ultimately concludes in the familiar vein: "Know, that nothing on earth is done without reason."[70]

In the second story the thesis is similar:

A cruel knight, who had long retained a devoted servant, was returning home through a grove, when he discovered he had lost thirty silver marks. Accusing the innocent servant of theft, the knight struck off the poor man's foot and left him to die. Hearing the groans of the man, a hermit went to his aid, heard his story, and carried him to his hut. Then, entering the oratory, the hermit reproached God for His want of justice, permitting an innocent man thus to lose his foot.

Though an angel appears to explain the Lord's equitable judgment upon a man who had maliciously spurned his mother, casting her out of a chariot by the same foot he himself later lost, the final answer is the only recourse of the medieval preacher:

"Don't speak an injustice against the Lord, for all His ways are truth and his judgments equity. Commit to memory what you have often read: The judgments of God are unfathomable. . . . Presume not to say anything against God. For God is a just judge and strong and long suffering; therefore do not say: Why did He make me, and then let me fall?"[71]

These stories from the *Gesta Romanorum,* we may be sure, resounded from the pulpits throughout the thirteenth century. The insistence that man accept on faith the unfathomable will of God, the reiterated apology for divine injustice, implies a considerable need of reassurance.

The spread of unbelief, though it affected only a minority, was not confined to any one people or country. As we have seen, according to Berthold of Regensburg and Caesarius of Heisterbach, some of the faithful of Germany often lapsed into doubts and indifference. Wolfram von Eschenbach allows Parzival to question God's justice, like those Christians of his time who could not reconcile with divine providence the existence of evil in the world.

Likewise we have seen that the French writers—Guiot de Provins, Gautier de Coincy, Etienne de Bourbon, the Monk of Froidmont, and Jean de Joinville—attest a spread of skepticism among high and low, noble and peasant alike. Philippe of

Novara, who lived most of his life in the Holy Land, adds his testimony in French literature to the spread of skeptical ideas he had noted. These were the pious writers, but there were secular writers also, like Matheolus and Pierre Cardinal and the author of *Aucassin et Nicolette,* lighthearted singers who wrote not with the intention to instruct or to improve morals so much as to entertain; and who also expressed a rational or a hedonistic attitude which challenged the Christian faith.

The English too, described by some writers as less subject than other people to corruption in the Church and blasphemy among the folk,[72] were often charged with skepticism. Giraldus Cambrensis, Matthew Paris, and Peter the Prior are among others who heaped abuse upon the people—clerks, schoolmen, and plain folk—who criticized Scripture and questioned dogmas.

Such indications of religious doubt as we have seen among all kinds and classes of thirteenth-century people suggest the curious contradictions and contrasts in a period that was noted for its inspiring expressions of a profoundly religious spirit. Coulton observed that it was an age of improvement and decay, optimism and despair;[73] and MacCulloch pointed out that these very centuries "which witnessed great personal devotion, the rise of the mendicant orders, the flourishing of scholasticism, the building of noble churches, the writing of the finest devotional prose and poetry, the rise of new forms of religious art, were thus also times, for many, of scepticism, free-thought, and sheer indifference."[74]

The Crusaders, Arabs, and Christianity

---

1. THE CRUSADES

RELIGIOUS SKEPTICISM OF THE MIDDLE AGES WAS, AS WE HAVE
seen, of various kinds and degrees: there was the skepticism
that came as a reaction to the moral degeneration of representatives of the Church; the skepticism that accompanied adversity
and hardship; the skepticism of the materialist; the involuntary
skepticism of the devout; the rational skepticism of those who
could neither accept nor explain the unjust distribution of
temporal favors. But a special kind of skepticism—a perplexity
as to God's will or power to fight His own battles—was swept
into Europe by the crusades. The movement of Christian
peoples to regain the Holy Sepulcher proved in the end
disastrous. The defeats of the crusaders, in their first attempts
to vanquish the Moslems, had early aroused criticism of God's
power. Long continued disaster produced a wave of dissatisfaction, fatalism, and infidelity.

It is neither possible nor desirable to describe here the
already well known Holy Wars of the Middle Ages, but Palmer
A. Throop[1] and Aziz Suryal Atiya,[2] on whom I have drawn for
some of the following material, can be consulted for excellent,
detailed summaries of the historical development of the crusading movement.

In a study of the thought of the Middle Ages, the crusades
deserve consideration as an act of devotion which was "the
perfect expression of one aspect of the medieval mind."[3] Even
a cursory review of the religious movement which, by the
concerted efforts of thousands, reached vast proportions shows
all the essential and often paradoxical qualities of medieval
peoples: their devotion to the Church, their relish for war,
their emotionalism, their boldness, their adventurous spirit,

their sentimentality and violence, courage and weakness, self-sacrifice and greed. 1619940

These qualities are at once apparent in the literature that grew directly out of the crusades, the successes and failures of which provoked alternate triumph and despair. Everyone is familiar with the names and feats of the first crusaders who entered Jerusalem in a tumult of glory, for generations have thrilled to the stories that came out of the early attempts to wrest the Holy Sepulcher from the infidel, romantic stories of chivalry which glorify bold knights and saints, brave deeds and miracles. These stories are dignified by the names of Raymond of Toulouse, Godfrey of Bouillon, Bohemund Prince of Antioch (all of the First Crusade), and Bernard of Clairvaux (of the Second), names that still command admiration.

These are the names which we all know. But our concern here is with those men, less well known when known at all, who strongly reacted against what in time appeared to be a lost cause. Successive defeats brought, along with despair over the losses, a storm of protest and criticism, and with the criticism a shaken faith. Such writings as reveal the doubts of men in their reflections upon God throughout this period illustrate a very human attitude, albeit one that was not always marked by an abiding trust in divine providence. If the evidence need not be taken as a sign of skepticism in the technical sense, it nevertheless proves that faith has its trials, trials which in the period of the crusades deeply disturbed the mind and soul.

Even the most zealous leaders were disheartened after the setbacks which followed the victorious First Crusade (1096-99). The official Church, to be sure, explained these appalling failures, like other calamities, as the retribution for sin. But such defenses were vaguely understood and failed to appease the disappointed hopes of even the most faithful. The pious Bernard, desolated by the defeat of the ill-advised Second Crusade (1147-49), found it difficult to reconcile the overwhelming losses with God's mercy:

The saint seems almost to have lost his faith. "Why," he cried, "has not God regarded our fasts, and appeared to know nothing

[35]

of our humiliations? With what patience is He now listening to the sacrilegious and blasphemous voices of the nations of Arabia, who accuse Him of having led His people into the desert that they might perish! All the world knows that the judgments of the Lord are just, but this is so profound an abyss that he is happy who has not been disgraced by it."[4]

Writing of the same campaign, the chronicler, William Archbishop of Tyre, though a devout Christian, looked upon the defeat with mingled feelings of despair and consternation:

Why is it, blessed Lord Jesus, that this people, so devoted to Thee, longing to adore the prints of Thy feet, desiring to kiss the revered places which Thou hast consecrated by Thy bodily presence, has suffered ruin at the hands of those who hate Thee? Truly, Thy judgments are a great abyss, and there is no one who can understand them.[5]

These early writers refrained, as later ones would not, from frankly challenging God's wisdom, but they could not forbear questioning His justice and mercy. The only answer lay in the inscrutability of the divine will.

Although the Christians conquered Acre in the Third Crusade (1189-92), it was with an incalculable loss of life and fortune; and the prestige of the crusades was impaired by stormy controversies and personal jealousies. The catastrophes inspired the kind of satirical verse that would later become more commonplace.

The Rabelaisian Monk of Montaudon (*fl.* 1200), a jovial fellow for all his holy robes, who preferred singing and laughter to kneeling endlessly in his cell, repudiated the vows he considered no longer binding in view of God's default:

But where the fleet of the Saracens
Is sailing You do not care at all,
For if it enters Acre,
The cruel Turk will profit thereby.
Foolish is he, who follows You into the quarrel.[6]

The close of the twelfth century was marked by the loss of its most romantic warrior, Richard Coeur-de-Lion, and the definite frustration of its purpose to win back the Holy Sepulcher. Crusading zeal began to wane in the thirteenth century; according to Ludlow, "the age had lost much of its religious zest."[7] By now it was a more disillusioned world in which men felt a discontent with things as they were, a discontent expressed in skepticism and indifference to spiritual things,[8] among the leaders as well as among the people.

It was shortly after the Fourth Crusade that the name of Simon de Montfort (1160-1218) was made illustrious in the crusade against the Albigenses in Southern France. Whatever his personal character, which lacked tolerance and humanity, Montfort's sincere devotion to the Cross cannot be questioned. But in his most violent struggle the tide of battle turned against him; finally blocked by the enemy, he fell into despair and angry complaint, as a contemporary poet tells us:

And the Count of Montfort is doleful and angered;
In a loud voice he cries: "God! why dost Thou hate me?"
"Lords," says the count, "knights, consider
This misfortune and how I am bewitched
So that now neither Church nor knowledge of letters is worth
    anything to me,
And the bishop cannot help me nor the legate aid me,
Nor is valor useful to me, nor my good deeds,
Nor does skill in arms, nor reason, nor generosity protect
    me." . . .
The count then comes to his brother, whom he loved,
And dismounts and utters bitter words:
"Dear brother," says the count, "at me and my companions
God has become angry, and He protects the mercenaries."[9]

When Montfort was killed by a huge stone rolled into the midst of the crusaders besieging Toulouse (1218), his men were thrown into confusion, and stung into resentful outcries over their loss:

In a loud voice they cry: "God, it is not just,
For Thou hast permitted the death of the count, and shame
    to him.
Surely he is foolish who defends Thee or is Thy servant,

When the count, who was so good and of so high adventure,
Is dead from [the blow of] a stone as if he had been Thine
    enemy.
And, moreover, Thy very kindred dost Thou prefer to torture
    and strike down."[10]

Montfort's son likewise was not reconciled to a God who
seemed indifferent to the fate of those who had served him
best:

"And God astonishes me in having been able to consent
To the death of His worthy son who was wont to serve Him.
Yet it is according to nature, as it seems to me,
That another father grieve when he sees his son die.
But God does not make a sign that it displeases Him or causes
    Him anguish.
When He had better kill [His enemies], He abases us."[11]

This sort of crusade, modeled theoretically at least on
crusades a century before and sanctioned by the Pope, seemed
designed to serve political and personal aims. As losses mounted
and selfish interests became more flagrant, it is easy to understand why men were disillusioned and embittered. Walter von
der Vogelweide (*fl.* 1215), most popular of all the German
minnesingers, began to fear that "God must be asleep, for the
infidels alone prosper."

Like Walter, Guglielmo Figeira, a troubadour in Toulouse
in 1229, reached both a learned and unlettered audience with
his popular songs. As the crusaders continued to suffer losses,
his lyrics were filled with bitterness. The Church recognized the
dangerous influence of such singers; if Figeira was not condemned by the Inquisition as has been stated by some historians
(though there is no clear evidence), he might well have been,
for he did not spare the papacy in his criticism:

> Rome, to the Saracens you do little harm,
> But the Greeks and Latins you massacre.[12]

Guillaume le Clerc also blamed the Holy See:

> Greatly must Rome be humiliated
> By the loss of Damietta.[13]

The debacle of Louis's crusade in 1250 brought forth a fresh storm of protest and a wave of skeptical expression, much of which Matthew Paris recorded:

Therefore many, whom a firm faith had not strengthened, began to waste away as much from despair and blasphemies as from hunger. And the faith of many, alas, began to waver, as they said to each other: "Why has Christ abandoned us, He on account of Whom and for Whom we have thus far been fighting? . . . Now however, what is more serious for all, our most Christian king, who was marvelously raised up from the dead, now along with all the nobility of France is exposed to disgraceful defeat. The Lord has become to us, as it were, an enemy. And He who is wont to be called Lord of the armies, now, oh grief! as if conquered many times, is despised by His enemies. What good to us then are our devotion, the prayers of the pious, the alms of our friends? Then is the law of Mahomet better than the law of Christ?" And thus on account of wavering faith, they repeated mad words, and Lent brought forth more sinners than penitents.[14]

The notably religious Austorc d'Orlac, in his grief over the death of St. Louis, was likewise stung into bitterness and doubt of God's justice:

Ah, God! why hast Thou brought such great misfortune
Upon our generous and courteous French king?
Why hast Thou permitted that he suffer so much shame?
For he strove to serve Thee as best he could,
    And placed his heart and mind
    To serve Thee night and day,
And to say and do only what would please Thee:
Evil reward hast Thou caused to befall him in this matter.

Ah! fair company, kind and courteous,
Who crossed the sea so splendidly armed,
Never shall we see you return—this is painful to me;
On which account throughout the world has spread great sorrow.
    Cursed be Alexandria,
    And cursed be all the clergy,
And cursed [be the] Turks who have made you fail:
God was wrong to give them the power to do it.

I see Christianity put completely to ruin by it;
Such a great loss I do not believe we have ever experienced;
Therefore it is reasonable for men henceforth to cease believing
   in God,
And to adore Mahomet instead,
   Tervagant and his company,
   Since God and [the] Holy Mary
Are willing that we be conquered against all right,
And cause unbelievers to remain with all honor.[15]

It was hard for those devoted to the Christian cause to understand the repeated losses of the crusaders. Why did the Saracens win? Why were most of the French nobility captured? Why did the pious Louis die? Throop's investigation reveals the rising discontent among Christian peoples: "One may find abundant evidence that men were actually asking these embarrassing questions. . . . Profound doubt had arisen from the very beginning of the crusades and as disaster followed disaster men came to wonder."[16]

Some were bitter; Salimbene said that the French, whose very pious king had met such ignominious defeat, were most bitter of all:

Those French who were left then in France were angered therefore; they presumed to blaspheme against Christ, moreover they went so far as to blaspheme the name of Christ which, above all names, should be blessed. For the Brothers Minor and Preachers in those days asked alms of the French in the name of Christ, but the French hissed through their teeth at these and when they saw them they would call some other beggar, give him money, and say: "Take this in the name of Mahomet, who is more powerful than Christ."[17]

Heretofore the sins of the leaders had been most often designated as the cause of defeat. But the success of the iniquitous Frederick II, followed by the failure of the embarrassingly pious St. Louis,[18] put churchmen in a superlatively uncomfortable position. To many the crusade seemed an increasingly fruitless venture.

Ricaut Bonomel (*fl.* 1265), himself a Templar in Palestine, had personally experienced the horror of the battlefield, and he had lost heart in the failing enterprise of the Christians. He could no longer believe in a God who was singularly indifferent to the battle that was being waged nobly in His name:

Sadness and pain have planted themselves in my heart
So that I have almost killed myself straightway
Or laid down the Cross which I had taken up
In honor of Him who was put on the Cross;
  For neither Cross nor faith protects or guides me
  Against the wicked Turks, whom God curse;
On the contrary it appears, as far as one can see,
That God wants to support them, to our destruction. . . .

Therefore, he is very foolish who fights against the Turks,
Since Jesus Christ does not stand against them at all;
That they conquered and are conquering, for this I am grieved—
The Franks and Tartars, Armenians and Persians;
  And they conquer us in our turn every day,
  For God sleeps who used to keep watch,
And Mahomet works with his power
And makes the Devil work.

It does not seem to me that He gives up for a time;
Rather He has sworn and said clearly
That no man who believes in Jesus Christ
Shall remain, if possible, in this land;
  Surely He will make a Mohammedan mosque
  Of the temple of the Holy Mary;
And, since His Son, who ought to have grief from this,
Wishes it or is pleased by this, it ought to please even us.[19]

Austorc de Segret, equally bewildered, wrote in a similar vein (1270-74):

  I do not know, so deeply confused am I,
  If God or the Devil has led us astray;
  For I see the Christians and their faith destroyed,
  And the Saracens have found support.[20]

Even the most faithful, seeing that the Christians were on the consistently losing side, began to ask questions. "I do not

[41]

know by what secret judgment God permits in our times frequent misfortunes to occur to crusaders fighting the Saracens," Humbert of Romans wrote to Gregory X about 1272.[21]

Among the lighthearted poets, also, exuberance gave way to lyrical complaint. Reconciled to this world and unperturbed about the next, they were not afraid to treat religious subjects with some levity; but the crusades they discussed with lively anger, taking personal issue with a God who seemed indifferent to the thousands who were dying for Him in the East. Daspol (*fl.* 1270) approached the problem with a practical argument and a patronizing air. He pretends to have attended, in a dream, a parliament in heaven and he describes his debate with God. He himself is bold in his accusations, his divine adversary weak and at a disadvantage in his own defense. To some of his pointed questions, the poet receives no response, and he challenges his opponent:

"You are wrong, God, and take another [i.e. the wrong] way,
For You give power to false people,
Who every day do deeds of pride and villainy,
Who do not believe or do anything good;
And You give them an abundance of gold and silver
So that Christians are discouraged by it,
For one cannot fight every day.

And You care little that You send us to slaughter.

My gracious Lord, Your royal glory
You could fulfill if You avoided the whole business without
    baseness;
Since You know that they all are disloyal,
Why do You permit them to reign in their wickedness?"[22]

From this time on, the crusades lost significance as a universal movement toward Christian unity, and the call to carry the Cross became less effectual. In his admirable study of the crusades in the later Middle Ages, Atiya emphasizes the fact that "the controversy between East and West began to have a new and different meaning. Devotion to the old cause, though still the ostensible pretext for waging holy war, was then mingled with many worldly interests."[23] Crusades had been too long a vital issue to lose all their influence even in the later Middle Ages, but earlier enthusiasm had yielded to indifference and less idealistic aims. Among other results of the crusades, the impetus to trade had been of considerable importance in establishing relations with other countries. And the large class of merchants could hardly, now, be expected to applaud the destruction and looting of eastern cities on which they depended for their most lucrative markets. Even men of the Church yielded to the temptation to stay at home to earn greater profits than could be had in the Holy Land. As Throop has observed, "The clergy no more than the laity could be stirred to give up their material interests for the sake of the crusade."[24] There was still response to the challenge to save the Christian heritage in the East, for there were still men genuinely devoted to the religious cause and there were always others who loved adventure. But the exalted faith that inspired the First Crusade had, after almost two centuries of discouragement and failure, lost much of its spontaneity. The wave of emotion that had carried ecstatic thousands into a hazardous undertaking had subsided and left many sobered. "The morale of Christendom had been sapped by despair and doubt."[25]

We can see in the literature that the crusades had not only had this sobering effect but had produced an attitude of fatalism and cynicism. The ultimate result, Throop concluded, was a fundamental change in religious belief: "Out of the extraordinary religious ferment of the thirteenth century there had grown a perception of the disparity between apostolic tradition and the practices of the medieval Church, between apostolic poverty and ecclesiastical wealth, between the peace preached by Christ and the holy war urged by his vicar. The decay of the crusades is inseparably bound up with this revision of Christian values."[26]

2. Skeptical Tendencies among the Learned

The disillusionment caused by the crusades was coincident with the sudden broadening of intellectual horizons, effected by the translations of Greek and Arabic philosophical, scientific, and medical works into Latin in the late twelfth and early thirteenth centuries. There was probably some connection between the crusade movement and the "Revival of Learning" of the Middle Ages.

The coincidence of the thirteenth century "Renaissance" with the period of the Crusades is striking, and it would be rash to deny any share in the outburst of intellectual energy which marks the thirteenth century to the new ideas and broadened outlook of those who, having gone on crusade, had seen the world of men and things in a way to which the society of the tenth and eleventh centuries was unaccustomed.[1]

If the failures of the crusades, and the acquaintance with non-Christian races and beliefs raised doubts among all classes of Christians, did the intellectual movement at the same time have a similar effect on the learned?

Skeptical and heretical ideas seemed to circulate among teachers and students in the universities and among physicians and other men of learning. Some medieval documents indicate to what source the men of the time attributed such ideas, which they blamed in general upon the study of natural philosophy. And the philosophy *par excellence* of the thirteenth century was Aristotle's. So dependent were the philosophers upon Aristotle that Etienne Gilson found medieval philosophy and Aristotelianism inseparable. "Retracer l'histoire de la philosophie au XIIIe siècle, époque classique de la philosophie médiévale, c'est définir les attitudes diverses qui furent adoptées dans les différents milieux philosophiques à l'égard de l'aristotélisme."[2]

Theologians criticized Aristotelian scholars for their tendency to credit Aristotle and infidel philosophers with pos-

[44]

sessing greater wisdom and authority than the Christian Fathers and the Bible and the saints. All through the thirteenth century, the records are replete with condemnation of the philosophers and teachers of philosophy. The implication is that the universities were centers of influence directed against orthodox teaching. Oxford, Cambridge, Paris, and Padua were blamed for encouraging thought which was in opposition to Christianity.

A number of rules and statutes, enacted to control the study of natural philosophy, indicate the growth of ideas considered harmful by the Church. As early as 1210 it was pronounced in Paris that "Neither the books of Aristotle on natural philosophy nor commentaries are to be read in Paris publicly or in secret and this we forbid under penalty of excommunication."[3] The statutes of the University of Paris in 1215 named the specific studies which were to be banned henceforth: "The books of Aristotle on metaphysics and natural philosophy, or summaries of them, are not to be read."[4]

Simon of Tournai, who was teaching at the University of Paris in 1201, is typical of freethinkers found in university circles. He was, by the middle of the century, accused of the most startling sacrileges. Thomas of Cantimpré said that Simon, given over to a reprobate mind, one day burst forth into execrable blasphemies:"There are three who divide the world with their sects and doctrines: Moses, Jesus, Mahomet. Moses, the first, made fools of the Jews, Jesus of the Christians, Mahomet of the pagans."[5] But Matthew Paris made it a more calumnious story:

And after the end [of a discussion] certain of those who were more familiar and more avid for learning approached, begging the master to let them write down these scientific discussions from his dictation; they said it would be shameful and an irreplaceable loss if the memory of such knowledge should perish. Exalted and flattered, he said with eyes raised and boldly laughing: "O little Jesus, little Jesus, how greatly I have strengthened and exalted thy doctrine in this discussion; assuredly, if I wished to malign and oppose it, by stronger reasons and arguments I could weaken it and render it unacceptable."[6]

Giraldus Cambrensis assures us Simon was a very learned man but was not a sound Christian, who, though he did not dare inveigh publicly against the faith, in private expressed his irreverent opinion to friends. One day, Giraldus says, Simon so far forgot himself in the presence of an acquaintance that he fell into a rage and cried out: "Omnipotent God! how long shall this superstitious sect of Christians and this newfangled invention endure?"[7] Talking his blasphemous way into medieval literature, Simon appears frequently, in the best commentaries of the period.

If the teachers of the universities engaged in such controversies, it is not surprising that a questioning spirit rose likewise among students. The effort to formulate theology, and even the mysteries of religion, in the language of Aristotelian philosophy, increased the doubts concerning such doctrines as that of transubstantiation. Much of the inquiry into the mysteries of the Church Caesarius attributed to the freethinking students at the University of Paris who "said that the body of Christ was not in the bread of the altar in any different way than in other bread and in everything; and that God had spoken in Ovid just as in Augustine."[8] But what could one expect of the young people? For there were teachers of Paris, he said, who "denied the resurrection of the body, saying that there was no Paradise or Hell."[9]

It was to curb such teachers that laws were passed to ensure orthodox training in the schools, like the regulation enforced at Paris in 1272: Statute of the faculty of arts against artists treating theological questions and that no one shall dare to determine against the faith questions which touch the faith as well as philosophy.[10] That "artists" did treat theological questions is attested by Humbert of Romans (1205-74) who charged the universities with "Seeking to know the incomprehensible, which cannot be clearly understood either by philosophical reasons or from holy scripture, as the mystery of the Trinity or sacrament of the Eucharist or predestination or knowledge of oneself and others."[11]

The very expositions intended to establish the existence of

[46]

God were deemed dangerous because of the negative implications. When "Utrum sit Deus" became a favorite thesis,[12] men of religion looked on with some uneasiness. Agnellus (c. 1195-1236), the Franciscan who built the Grey Friars' School, hearing at Oxford such disputations among the brothers, mourned over the futile dialectics: "Woe is me, woe is me! Simple brothers enter Heaven, while learned brothers dispute whether there be a God at all!"[13]

That questions regarding Church doctrine had arisen in the minds of students and teachers alike is evident in the university records. A letter addressed to the Pope by Stephen of Tournai[14] is filled with invectives against the new learning which encouraged controversy over religious issues:

People publicly dispute against the sacred canons regarding the incomprehensible deity; verbose flesh and blood irreverently litigates concerning the incarnation of the Word. The indivisible Trinity is cut up and is plucked apart in public places, so that now there are as many errors as doctors, as many scandals as classrooms, as many blasphemies as public squares. . . . All these things, Father, need the hand of apostolic correction.[15]

The Bishop of Paris, in 1270, listed, among thirteen counts against the universities, independence of Church law and the teaching of many errors according to principles of natural philosophy:

That the soul, which is the form of man as man, becomes corrupt when the body has become corrupt.

That the soul, when it has separated from the body after death, does not suffer from corporeal fire.

That human actions are not ruled by the providence of God.[16]

The bishop demanded condemnation and punishment for whoever taught or knowingly asserted these heresies.

St. Bonaventure (1221-74) was one of the churchmen who most bitterly attacked the enthusiasm for natural philosophy as such, commending the early Church for burning the books of philosophy.[17] That he looked upon the cult of pagan and infidel philosophy as a danger to Christian teaching is made apparent in frequent critical references to philosophy in his *Hexaemeron*:

Moreover, to descend to philosophy is the greatest danger. . . . Whence masters should be on their guard, and not unduly recommend and value the sayings of the philosophers, lest by this occasion the people go back into Egypt, or by their example abandon the waters of Siloah, in which is the highest perfection, and rush into the waters of the philosophers, in which is eternal deception.[18]

Much of this kind of criticism was aimed directly at the Arabs and "Arabists" because of what Gilson calls the "inevitable conflict between Arab philosophy and Christian theology."[19] A further charge against the Arabs was that they were responsible for bringing Greek philosophy also to the western world. "And when we examine the great motive force of the thirteenth century 'Revival of Learning' it is Aristotle from whom the impulse proceeded, and Aristotle first brought back to the West by way of Spain and the Moorish versions of his works."[20]

Frederick II was one of those who were attacked for devotion to Arabic culture and learning, his interest in which won him many charges of infidelity. Reared in Palermo, where he lived in luxury that was half oriental and half western, he was steeped in eastern culture. There "Greek and Arabic learning were united,"[21] and amidst the remains of Moslem civilization he was afforded the opportunity to associate with Arabian scholars and perhaps even to learn something of their language. It is certain that he knew much about their philosophy.

For Frederick, as ruler of the Holy Roman Empire and King of Naples and Sicily, had occasion to negotiate with the eastern leaders, with whom he discussed philosophical as well as political matters. Like all other medieval men of high intelligence, Frederick was consumed with interest in Aristotle, especially through the Arabs, whom he frequently questioned about philosophical problems. He wrote to Ibn-Sabin (*b.* 1218):

[48]

"The wise Aristotle, in all his writings, states clearly the existence of the world *ab aeterno*. There is no doubt he had this opinion. Nevertheless, if he demonstrated it, what are his arguments; if not, of what sort is his reasoning on the subject? . . . What is the nature of the soul? What is the sign of its immortality? Is the soul immortal?"[22]

Frederick's materialistic attitude was not expressed by questioning alone; it was manifested in actual experiments in which, like a scientist, he put religion to the test—as when he had a man placed in a hermetically sealed cask which, when opened, revealed a corpse but no traces of a soul![23]

Scarcely a religious man of the age but had his say regarding the reprehensible Frederick. Albert of Bohemia (1183?-1258) wrote a long tract against the Emperor, not omitting his lack of faith:

Moreover, it is not to be wondered at, if he promiscuously and without discretion destroys men unjustly, since he does not fear temporal punishment and, even less, eternal punishment; according to him, as his intimates claim, the soul of man dies with the body, like the heresy of the Sadducees, who did not believe there is a future resurrection and that an angel or spirit exists. In truth, to such men, all divine worship, laws of Christ, and the Gospels are empty and vain.[24]

Gregory IX repeatedly denounced his materialistic attitude:

Moreover, he dared clearly to affirm or rather to say falsely that all are fools who believe that God, who created nature and all the world, could be born of a Virgin. . . . And [he says] one must believe nothing except what he can see and prove by natural reason. By these and many other such words and deeds he has attacked and still attacks the Catholic faith, as, it is fitting and expedient, can be clearly proved in this time and place.[25]

Salimbene tells us that Frederick searched the Scripture to show that there was no life after death.[26] But he could so greatly appreciate Frederick's genius that he mourned, rather than condemned, his recalcitrance to the Church:

Note that Frederick almost always chose to have discord with the Church and has repeatedly assailed it which sustained, protected, and exalted him. Of faith in God he had none. He was a hostile man, sly, avaricious, dissolute, wicked, wrathful. And yet he was a mighty man and, when he wished to show his goodness and faithfulness, was sympathetic, pleasant, charming, diligent; he could read, write, and sing and make up songs and lyrics; he was a handsome man and well formed, but medium in height. . . . He could speak many different languages. . . . If he had been a good Catholic and esteemed God and the Church and his soul, he would have had few emperors his equal in the world.[27]

(Later Salimbene's own faith wavered and after 1260, having taken up and then put aside the heretical doctrine of Joachism, he declared that he was disposed to believe nothing except what he should see.)[28]

In view of Frederick's reputation, it is natural that he should have become associated with the hypothetical book known as *The Three Impostors* (*De Tribus Impostoribus*). Since the twelfth century there had circulated a story that there was such a book which, it was assumed, described all religions as false. No one had ever seen the book, but the persistence of the legend of its existence indicates the vitality of the heretical ideas with which it supposedly was concerned. The readiness to attribute the work to every freethinker from Averroes on[29] indicates the stigma attached to the story from early times. Matthew Paris is one of the chroniclers who attributed to Frederick the ideas which the book was said to contain. Commenting on Frederick's reputed character of impiety, Matthew Paris dilated on his alliance with the Saracens:

It was charged against him that he wavered in the Catholic faith and uttered words from which could be found out not only his weakness in faith but indeed an execrable amount of heresy and blasphemy. It was reported he had said, though perhaps it should not be repeated, that three deceivers, craftily and cunningly in order that they might rule the world, had completely led the universe of contemporary people astray, namely Moses,

[50]

Jesus, and Mahomet; and that he had put forth certain ravings about the Eucharist. Far, far be it from any discreet man to open his mouth and utter such mad blasphemy. It was also said by his rivals that the Emperor Frederick himself was more in accord with the law of Mahomet than that of Jesus Christ. . . . And it was rumored among the people, which God forbid in so great a prince, that for a long time he was himself an ally of the Saracens and was more a friend to them than to Christians.[30]

The suspicion of the new natural philosophy expressed by the pious vented itself particularly in attacks on the Arab philosopher, Averroes, a scholar learned in theology, medicine, jurisprudence, astronomy, and mathematics as well as philosophy. He came to symbolize the error of setting philosophy over revealed Christian doctrine chiefly because his commentaries on Aristotle, the best and most accurate then available, were used universally as the standard guide to the understanding of Aristotle's thought. Averroism was not in itself anti-Christian; it was what Professor Sarton describes as "Aristotelian positivism," which by a series of misunderstandings became distorted. "Among other things, Averroism had come to mean free thought in the sense of irreligion; its supporters were accused of questioning the fundamental doctrines of the church, especially of doubting the dogmas of creation and of the immortality of the soul."[31] And Frederick did a great deal to spread Arabic learning throughout the world. "Frederick II. set great store on the commentaries of Averroës and did much to popularize them: by the middle of the thirteenth century Paris was in possession of all the writings of Averroës except his commentaries on the *Organon* and his *Destructio Destructionis*."[32]

Fourteenth-century theologians and philosophers carried on the conflict with Arabism. Groote (1340-84), according to Thomas à Kempis in the *Vita Gerardi Magni,* warned a young man, who asked his advice about an opportunity to go to Paris to study, that he would risk losing his faith, for Paris had been ruined by philosophy.[33]

In a fourteenth-century collection of pious tales, *Le Tombel*

[51]

de Chartrose, the poet gives over his preface and epilogues to serious reflections. Here he exercises a faculty of criticism that throws light on many problems of the time. Along with moral counsel and an enumeration of current evils, we find a protest against acceptance of Averroes:

> Alas! see how the prophecy
> Has in our time been fulfilled,
> When rather are words heard
> Of the evil Averroes,
> Who was with all his power
> An enemy of our faith,
> Who chose the life and death of the beast;
> For no one lends his ears
> To hear words of the Bible.[34]

If criticism of a doctrine indicates the prevalence of that doctrine, the extent of Arabic thought in Italy may be measured by the warmth of Petrarch's aversion to it. To Petrarch the humanist, the Arabs seemed crude and medieval. He made the sweeping assertion that he hated the whole race, from whom he firmly believed nothing good could possibly come.[35] He carried his distaste so far that he even refused to be treated by Arabian doctors or to employ remedies with Arabian names.

Petrarch was unsympathetic toward "scientific philosophers" in general and toward Averroes in particular. He wrote to his friend Luigi Marsigli, an Augustinian monk:

Lastly, I beg that as soon as you have arrived, speak out—and I trust quickly—against that mad dog Averroes, who, driven by unspeakable frenzy, barks against his Lord Christ and against the Catholic faith. As you know, I had already started to collect their blasphemies from everywhere, but an always enormous and now more habitual employment, not to mention lack of time as well as knowledge, holds me back. Applying yourself with all the force and vigor of your genius to an affair impiously overlooked by many great men, write a little work and dedicate it to me, whether I am living then or die meanwhile.[36]

His dislike for Averroes represents Petrarch's dislike for all scholars who preferred the authority of pagan philosophers to the authority of the Bible and the Church and St. Augustine.

Once he entertained in his library at Venice a philosopher, an Arabist who, as the writer later said in a letter to Boccaccio, was like all those who as modern thinkers felt obliged to harp against simple Christian teaching.

Recently there was here in my library one of these, who was not even dressed in the religious habit—though to be a Christian the most important thing is religious feeling alone— one of these I say, however, who in the modern custom of philosophers believe they have done nothing unless they rant against Christ and the holy doctrine of Christ. When I uttered to him I know not what from Holy Scriptures, he, boiling with rage, his nature made ugly by anger, and with contemptible arrogance disfiguring his brow, said:

"Keep your little Church Fathers. As for me, I have someone to follow and I know in whom I have believed."

I replied: "You have used the words of the Apostle, and would that you were willing to use them faithfully."

"That Apostle of yours," he said, "was an author of words and a madman."

"You answer like the best philosopher," I replied.

. . . He burst into sickening laughter, exclaiming: "Well, be a good Christian; as for me, I believe none of all these things. Your Paul and your Augustine and all the others you preach about were the most garrulous men. Would that you could endure Averroes so that you might see how much superior he is to these good-for-nothings of yours."[37]

When Petrarch tells us he could hardly contain his anger, we wonder how well he succeeded if, as he declares, he took the man by the coat and put him out bodily. Another such philosopher once dared to say to Petrarch:

"Alas! what a shame that such a genius has been ensnared by groundless fables. . . . Yes, truly, you are a fool if you believe thus as you say. But I expect better things of you."[38]

Furious, Petrarch in recounting the incident to Boccaccio exclaims: "What might he expect of me but to be, along with him, one who condemns piety in silence!"[39] History fails to tell whether this man also suffered an indignity, though we are left in no doubt as to what his host thought of him.

Petrarch's tone is often scornful when he refers to these devotees of Arabic philosophy, whose attacks on Christianity, he asserted, only strengthened his own faith.

If they were not more terrified by human than by divine punishment, they would dare to attack not only the creation of the world according to Plato in the Timaeus but the Genesis of Moses, and the Catholic faith, and all the most sacred and wholesome dogmas of Christ. When they lose this fear and banish their masters, they strike at truth and piety, laughing at Christ in secret corners and adoring Aristotle whom they do not understand.[40]

Boccaccio was less humanistic but more human than his contemporary Petrarch. An accomplished, enthusiastic scholar, he won his place in world literature as the author of the *Decameron,* the work which brings his name into this study. From a thirteenth-century collection, *Il Novellino,* Boccaccio took the story of "The Three Rings," and he made of it a narrative which he included in the *Decameron.*[41] It is doubtless this story that won for him also the suspicion of having written *The Three Impostors.*

The story of "The Three Rings," an ancient parable with a long history, appeared frequently in the thirteenth century. Its last medieval version, written by Boccaccio, is the culmination of three streams of development: Jewish, Christian, and Arabic. Its originator was probably a Jew in Spain, and the earliest Jewish adaptation already sounded a note of skepticism which would become more marked in later versions, especially in Italian. Gaston Paris attributed this skepticism chiefly to the unbelief growing out of the failure of the crusades and the concurrent influence of Mohammedan thought.

The lesson of skepticism which evolves out of the story, more sharply in the Italian than in the early form, could have been overlooked at least by one or another of those who accepted it;

but if we consider in what times and in what milieu it was produced, we cannot doubt that it was perfectly understood by most people, as it certainly was by Boccaccio, the last narrator. Skepticism sprang up, in fact, as has already been indicated, as much from the failure of the crusades in the Holy Land as from the relations between Christians and Moslems: it had been seen that there was, besides the Jews, another sect of men, who displayed culture, virtues, and a power that Christian effort had not vanquished; who believed, like the Christians and Jews, in one God, who like them held the Bible as a sacred book, and who declared the Christian dogmas contrary to the Bible and to the notion of one God. That the Saracens or Jews had the truth could not be believed, or at least very little; but was it certain that the Christians had it, or that it had been revealed to anyone at all? Some did not stop at doubt: they went so far as to express the rudest denial.[42]

A man of independent judgment, Boccaccio took up the legend of Jewish origin and skilfully fashioned it into a simple tale with implications which would long disturb the Christian world.

Saladin, calling before him a rich Jew, thought to trick the old man into a confession that would cost him the repudiation of his faith or the forfeit of his fortune—a sum that the ruler sorely needed. "Which of the three religions, Christianity, Islam, or Judaism," the wily Saladin asked, "is best?" The wise old man reflected; if he named Judaism, he knew he would pay the penalty the ruler wanted to exact; if he made any other answer, it would be to betray his own faith.

So, measuring his words carefully, he replied by telling the parable of a man who had three sons, all of whom he loved alike. Having but one very costly ring which one of the sons would inherit, the father had two rings fashioned so like the original that no one could tell the difference. Then he secretly gave the rings to the three boys, each of whom believed he owned the genuine ring. "So it is with the three religions," concluded the old man. "Each man believes his own faith is genuine, and only the Father knows which is the true one."

The moral is obvious, but there was no less difficulty in

convincing the fourteenth century of its importance than the twentieth. The implication that tolerance of Islam and Judaism should be based not on good will and charity but the possibility that Christianity was not after all the true religion was radical. In the Italian version the prince was named Saladin, and this was not by chance, for traditionally Saladin was interested in such questions and was known for tolerance and justice.

It may not be by chance, either, that Italy, the center of medieval medicine, became also a center of Arabic philosophy and of fourteenth-century skepticism, for there was a curious relationship between practitioners of medicine, followers of Arabic thought, and critics of religion. So notoriously critical was the spirit among members of the medical faculties that it gave rise to a proverb well known in the Middle Ages: "Ubi tres medici, duo athei." Since Averroes himself studied medicine and wrote treatises on the subject, there was good reason for the medieval physician's familiarity with Averroes' work.

Petrarch, with an abhorrence for both doctors and Arabs, hardly drew a line between the two. In the long *Invective against a Certain Doctor,* he describes the profession as lacking in cultural tastes, scornful of poetry, grasping, appreciative only of material values, and preferring Averroes to Christ.

Another tie that bound the medieval physician to the Arab was the dependence of medical practice upon astrology, a field to which the Arabs had made the most notable contributions. It is not a literary accident that Chaucer described his Doctor of Physic as one whose "studie was but litel on the Bible," a fact whose significance Professor Tupper, among others, has noted:

So far is Chaucer from availing himself of a merely conventional gird at the traditional skepticism of the tribe of physicians that the true implication of the line is revealed only by a study of contemporary unfaith. No verse in all the Prologue has a more definite connotation. The Doctor's "study was but little on the Bible," not because he is a typical physician of any or every age, but because he is a fourteenth-century Arabist and astrologer.[43]

[56]

It is not strange, then, that the physician of the *Canterbury Tales* knew Averroes.

That Aristotle, as transmitted through Arabic and Jewish translations, made a strong appeal to scholars of the thirteenth and fourteenth centuries there is no doubt. A library left in the fifteenth century by John of Marcanuova to the abbey of St. John in Verdara, now at St. Mark's, is almost exclusively composed of Averroes' works. And the movement was by no means short-lived: the Latin editions of the Commentaries between 1480 and 1580 are said to number about a hundred.[44]

It is easy to exaggerate the influence that natural philosophy had on the medieval mind. The philosophers themselves accepted the orthodox creed; they were more interested in furthering intellectual inquiry than corrupting the faith, which they often considered, indeed, as a matter apart from philosophy. It is not believed that the philosophers ever, in their theories, presented a threat to the Church, or that their influence went very far beyond scholarly circles. But that some of them were open to charges of skepticism is evident in the frequent expression of fears and hatreds in the thirteenth- and fourteenth-century writings of conservative theologians and religious people outside the universities.

3.   The Fourteenth Century

THE AGE OF CHAUCER SAW NO SUBSIDENCE IN THE WAVE OF religious discontent. In view of the many thirteenth-century testimonies to the existence of a spirit of questioning and denial, it is curious to find Professor Sarton speaking of the fourteenth century as "an age of incipient doubts, of restlessness and rebellion."[1] Certainly the challenge to the authority of the Church in matters of thought and discipline was nothing new, but there were certain new causes for disturbance and certain new forms of revolt.

The great triumphs of scholasticism in the reconciliation of reason and dogma had already been achieved, and seemed to leave little for succeeding generations except endless debates over subtleties beyond the comprehension of any but the most acute intellects. The monastic clergy, so far at least as the popular impression went, were given over to a life of lazy self-indulgence, while the friars, of whom so much had been expected in the days of St. Francis and St. Dominic, had become a byword for hypocrisy. The issuing of papal indulgences and the sale of saints' relics were widely accompanied by fraud. For seventy years the papal see was fixed at Avignon (1307-77), and roused violent criticism by its subservience to French policy and the scandalous license of the papal court. All these factors produced a vigorous anticlericalism among the laity, even among the most devout. Those who would not dream of attacking the doctrines of the Church regarding faith and morals were shocked by the morals of her ministers. When at the end of the century Europe was split into warring factions by the Great Schism, and two popes claimed to be vicars of Christ on earth, men were naturally moved to inquire not only whether the Church had betrayed her Master by her conduct

[58]

but also whether she could be relied on to speak with the voice of God.

Nowhere is the anticlericalism of the period expressed more plainly than in the General Prologue of the *Canterbury Tales*. The revolt against the authority of the Pope found its most formidable expression in the Lollard movement which numbered among its adherents some of Chaucer's intimate friends. These, however, were but the more conspicuous manifestations of the questioning and challenging spirit of Chaucer's England.

London, with its thirty-five thousands,[2] was the center of English culture and learning. Walsingham (d. 1422?), the monk of St. Albans, was closely connected with the court as royal historiographer, and his painstaking compilation of facts gives us a detailed picture of contemporary conditions. When he refers to Londoners in 1392 as the "most unbelieving in God," and enumerates the evils of the time, we can see that he was not cheerful about the spiritual well-being of his fellow countrymen.

They [Londoners] were indeed at that time among almost all nations of peoples the most exalted, most arrogant, and most covetous, and most unbelieving in God and the old traditions. . . . So much grew their arrogance that they dared establish laws by which they vexed, oppressed, and harassed visitors from adjacent cities and provinces against all human propriety, God, and justice.[3]

With great rhetorical skill, Walsingham, slyly pretending to gloss over the Londoners' defects, damns them by implication in a list of evils that he (ostensibly) refuses to describe:

I omit their inhumanity, I am silent on their greediness, I conceal their lack of faith, I pass over their maliciousness, which they waywardly exercised upon visiting peoples.

More pointedly, he singles out those failings he had himself observed in people of the city, especially their offenses against the Church, which the lower classes—with new boldness lent

[59]

by an increasing urge for freedom—blamed on the upper classes.

Some ascribed the cause of evils to the sins of the lords, who lacked faith in God; for certain of these believed, as it was claimed, there was no God, there was no Sacrament of the altar, there was no resurrection after death; but that, as the animal dies, so also ends man.[4]

True, Walsingham saw the world through the eyes of a churchman. A man of unremittingly strict religious standards and zealous piety is likely to find in every transgression that comes to his attention some form of heresy, and this monk of St. Albans could have exaggerated the situation. But his charge against the people of London is not without the support of other writers, cleric and secular alike. The cumulative force of evidence found in contemporary works gives a certain weight to the statement even of an alarmist like Walsingham.

For there were others, about the same time, who expressed equal concern over the "frequency with which dogmas of the Church were now criticised by the man in the street," as Coulton said in commenting on *Piers Plowman*.[5] Certainly no man of the time was more strongly moved by the ills of society than was William Langland (1330?-1400?). Sternly pious, sincere and earnest, Langland, in rugged, impetuous lines, criticized the lust and evil of the city. He wrestled endlessly with doubts and despair, and by middle-age was a humbled and disillusioned man. But this poet who at forty went about singing dirges for a few pennies, by the world's standards a failure, won wide approval, for there seems to have been a popular acceptance of his brilliantly imaginative and deeply moral allegory.[6]

Of the people and for the people, the satirist-preacher gives us what is probably the best index we have of the mind of the average Englishman of the fourteenth century. In *Piers Plowman* the poet complains about the criticism of dogmas by laymen. From now on till the sixteenth century there would be what Coulton noted as an "increasing evidence of a more voluntary popular skepticism."[7] Not unaware of the shortcomings of the poor over whose poverty and oppression he yearned passionately, Langland placed the burden of blame upon the rich for the prevalence of unbelief, for their impious questionings which "make men disbelieve that reflect much on their words."

Now is the manere atte mete   when mynstralles ben stylle,
The lewede a-yens the lered   the holy lore to dispute,
And tellen of the trinite   how two slowe the thridde,
And brynge forth ballede resones   and taken Bernarde to witnesse,
And putteth forth presompcions   to preouen the sothe.
Thus thei dreuelen atte deyes   the deyte to knowe,
And gnawen god with gorge   when here guttes fullen.
    Ac the carful mai crie   and quaken atte yate,
Bothe a-fyngred and a-furst   and for defaute spille,
Ys non so hende to haue hym yn   bote hote hym go ther god is!

                     (PP, C, XII, 35-44)

There were rich men, then, who dared to speak in mockery of two members of the Trinity killing the third, and to order beggars to go to God for relief.

The fearless Wyclif(d. 1384) included the hypocrisy of a corrupt clergy as one of the chief causes of the wavering faith of the common people. Like Langland, Wyclif led a life of sternly uncompromising piety and dedicated his mind and energy to fighting against unchristian living. The two men had in common a hatred of hypocrisy and greed, which they held to be the outstanding causes of evil, and they constantly berated the clergy for abuses of their office. In his great religious tract, the *Trialogus,* his "theological bequest"[8] to the world, Wyclif did not mince words:

I do not doubt but that our religious in private are so unbelieving, valuing their own proofs in this respect, for all such people are disobedient to the law of the Gospels, since they value their own false signs more than the fruit of the faith which is taught in the law of the Gospels.[9]

Wyclif vigorously criticized the friars for the practice—too often a purely mercenary one—of presuming to grant a share of their own merit by letters to penitents. He not only accused them of thus spreading infidelity but strongly implied that they themselves had too little merit to share:

It seems to be more than a presumption of the devil to grant a share of the merit of a man who is himself a hypocrite. . . . How then does this heresy fail to give an occasion of generally falling in the way [of a believer]? . . . Indeed this heresy of the friars is supposed to be the cause why the faith among laymen thus wavers.[10]

The sermons of the average preacher took such people as all these sternly to task:

But off euery estate they [thees worldely clerkes, Bisshopes, Abbotes and Priours] take luste and ese, and putte ffro hem the travaylle, and takyth profytes that shulden kome to trewe men, the which lyff and evyll ensample off hem hath be so longe vicious that alle the commone peple, both lordes and symple comvnes, beth now so vicious and enfecte thurh boldeship off her synne, that vneth eny man dredith god ne the devyll.[11]

When we turn to France, we find that Guillaume le Maire, distinguished Bishop of Angers between 1291 and 1317, is a witness to the same religious indifference in his own country:

Wherefore it happens that on those holy days, on which especially God should be worshiped, the Devil is worshiped; churches remain empty; courts, taverns, and work places resound with quarrels, tumults, blasphemies, perjuries; and there crimes of almost all kinds are perpetrated. From these things it follows that the law of God, the articles of the faith and other things that pertain to the religion of the Christian faith and the salvation of souls are, as it were, completely unknown by the faithful. Therefore God is blasphemed, the Devil is revered, souls are being lost, the Catholic faith is being wounded; whence it would be very necessary to apply a sound remedy upon so great errors and abuses.[12]

As mild mannered a writer as the author of *Le Mireour du monde* (1352-53?) was harsh with the materialists who would believe only what they could see. This gentle Christian philosopher, who seemed to live apart from a stormy world, reflected upon the morals of men with infinite patience and sympathy. There is a kind of beauty in the variety of images he uses to point up his moralistic discussion, and a certain charm in his enthusiasm over his exploration of the human heart. In striking contrast to his general spirit of benign tolerance and charity is the tone he assumes in dealing with Christians whose only sin seemed to be doubt of the mysteries they could not understand. He blamed pride for their unbelief and vain disputation.

The greatest possible pride is unbelief. Is it not great pride when a peasant who does not even know his paternoster aright believes he knows more of divinity than all the clerks of Paris, and thinks he is of greater worth than all the monks of Citeaux and will not believe that God knows how to do anything on earth that he cannot understand?[13]

We find, besides general expressions of wavering faith, specific criticism of doctrine. Of most vital concern, since the most profound religious aspiration of the human heart has always reached toward a life beyond life, was the loss of faith in immortality. In this form of unbelief we see both pathos and bravado: some people could not believe what they earnestly wanted to;[14] others arrogantly said that the doctrine of immortality had been invented "to strike terror into men and restrain them from rash and daring deeds."[15]

Even the gentle, pious Dame Juliana of Norwich confessed the sin of doubt. Said to have been born about 1342, Juliana was probably a Benedictine nun belonging to Carrow, Norwich, where she lived in an anchorage of the churchyard of St. Julian.[16] Yearning for a profound religious experience, Juliana earnestly prayed that she might fall ill "so hard as to the death" in order to learn contrition, compassion, and longing for God. In her thirtieth year, such an illness came upon her, during which she had sixteen revelations that she set down in a charming little book. Her desire to recover and "live more to the worship of God because of that sicknes" was granted in full measure, since she was still living in 1413.[17]

Among the few women writers of the Middle Ages, Juliana is one of the most appealing religious figures of the time. Her faith, despite troubled doubts, remained unshaken, "for it is the most unpossible [thing] that may [be], that we should seek mercy and grace, and not have it."[18] In an age when the religious life was often regarded as grim and penitential, Juliana's happy spirit of optimism is refreshing. Every page of her work is lightened with such words as *hope, joy, delight, brightness, merry, glad,* which come so often to her pen: "for I understood that we may laugh in comforting of our self, and joying in God."[19]

It was this buoyant spirit which brought to Juliana's mind a question concerning the teaching of the Church, for she could not wholly reconcile the doctrine of damnation with a merciful God. If, as Holy Church teaches, the sinners shall be damned, then how believe God's words that had come to her in a vision?

'I may make all thing well; and I can make all thing well; and I shall make all thing well; and I will make all thing well; and thou shalt see thyself that all manner of thing shall be well.'[20]

But "yet oftentimes our trust is not full; for we be not sure that God heareth us . . . for thus have I felt by my self."[21]

Juliana's attitude toward damnation was in opposition to the often heard sermons on fire and brimstone; her declaration that in her direct spiritual experience nothing could be so impossible as an angry, avenging God is far from the most widely accepted teaching of her time. Coulton saw in her humanitarian view "a strong tendency to escape from the cruel theology . . . commonly preached and understood."[22]

Closely related to the doctrine of damnation is the fate of the "righteous heathen." Common sense and humanitarianism raised a question in many minds about salvation for those good men born in the pre-Christian era who, unable to benefit from Christian teaching, were therefore through no fault of their own excluded from the Christian paradise. R. W. Chambers made a careful study of this problem in his admirable essay, "Long Will, Dante, and the Righteous Heathen."[23] Many medieval authorities taught (and some moderns still teach) that only by Christian baptism can man save his soul. Even John Wyclif, who opposed the established Church on many issues of doctrine and government, stated emphatically that there were not many churches but only one, the catholic (universal) Church, outside of which there was no salvation or remission of sins.[24] According to ecclesiastical authority, such men as Virgil, Cato, Aristotle, Plato were lost to the life eternal by the accident of having been born before Christ. The break with such belief was manifested by medieval writers who dealt in one way or another with the question of salvation on the basis of personal merit rather than Christian baptism.

The precedent had been set for the fourteenth century by Thomas Aquinas (1225?-74), the scholastic philosopher who exercised greater influence on the Western Church than any theologian after Augustine. He was fully aware of the complexity of this problem and stated the case of the "heretic-born" (that is, anyone born at a time or place that precluded knowledge of Christianity) as depending on individual will and faith.

. . . But before Christ's coming . . . men were incorporated in Christ by faith alone, as Gregory says (*Moral.* iv), together with the offering of sacrifices, by means of which the Fathers of old made profession of their faith.[25]

If, however, some were saved without receiving any revelation, they were not saved without faith in a Mediator, for, though they did not believe in Him explicitly, they did, nevertheless, have implicit faith through believing in Divine providence, since they believed that God would deliver Mankind in whatever way was pleasing to Him.[26]

Dante followed St. Thomas but seemed never to solve the problem to his own satisfaction. Dante's perplexity is apparent in his frequent consideration of virtuous pagans and the way he dealt with them. He was forced to place in Limbo those "men of much worth" who lived before Christ and were lost "for such defects, and for no other fault," condemned to live in desire without hope. Yet we find Cato in Purgatory and Ripheus in Paradise.

It is striking that Dante again introduces the whole problem in the *Paradiso,* for such a disturbed state of mind would seem to belong to a lesser sphere. It is a surprise to find so troubled a thought intruding into the poet's final vision, filled as it is with the glorious light of spiritual joy awarded to the pure in heart as a consummation of a life of righteousness. Yet Dante's reference to a theological issue here, near the climax of his great work, indicates the poet's long struggle with the problem of justice and his passionate desire to justify the will of God. Here in the heaven of justice, yearning to solve the mystery of the exclusion of noble but unchristian souls from salvation, Dante asks the question that he says "hath been to me a fast of so long date." Wicksteed has spoken of "the mental anguish which throbs through the appeal in this present passage."[27] The intensity of feeling in the poet's appeal makes it almost a cry of protest against divine will:

> . . . 'A man is born upon the bank of Indus and there is none to tell of Christ, nor none to read, nor none to write;
>
> and all his volitions and his deeds are good so far as human reason seeth, sinless in life or in discourse.
>
> He dieth unbaptized and without faith; where is that justice which condemneth him? where is his fault, in that he not be-lieves?'
>
> (*Par,* xix)

The eagle reproves the poet: "Now who art thou who wouldst sit upon the seat to judge?"

> . . . "To this realm ne'er rose one who believed not in Christ, neither before nor after he was nailed unto the tree."
>
> (*Par,* xix)

Yet this unqualified judgment is softened by a ray of hope— and it is very near heresy:

[66]

"But see, many cry Christ, Christ, who at the judgment shall be far less near to him than such as know not Christ."

(*Par,* xix)

Even the orthodox Sacchetti, in his *Sermoni,* emphatically rejected the damnation of the righteous heathen.

Can a man who happens to live and to have been born a pagan or a Saracen be saved, if he has not received baptism? I answer yes, if he lives reasonably and justly, doing to others what he would have done unto him. . . . I say to you that faith and good will make all men worthy of salvation.[28]

Rulman Merswin was another who took advantage of the slight concession that St. Thomas had made. A Jewish banker who had been converted to the faith (*c.* 1350), he must have come in contact with many good people who by Christian law would be condemned. It was his thesis therefore that any good Jew or heathen who lived earnestly by the faith in which he was born but became willing to accept another, better creed might, even without baptism, be saved at the very moment of death:

. . . thus when God findeth a very righteous, good heathen or a very righteous, good Jew, what doth God then? I will tell thee: God, who cannot give up His joyous love and His boundless mercy, cometh to his help. I will tell thee: God findeth many secret ways so that these well-wishing, God-fearing men not be lost, at whatever end of the wide world they are. . . . When this good heathen or this good Jew cometh to his last, then cometh God ever to his aid and enlighteneth him with the Christian faith to such an extent that he longeth for it with all his heart. . . . I will tell thee what God doth then: God goeth and baptizeth him on account of his good desire and his bitter death. Thou shalt know that many of these good heathens and good Jews are in eternal life, all of whom came there in such a way.[29]

Chaucer's countrymen, too, were wrestling with the problem. In Langland's *Piers Plowman,* the question of salvation for the righteous heathen raised such difficulties that Langland himself, in the earlier version at least, ventured no answer. The A-text (1373?) breaks off sharply and leaves the question unresolved. Chambers believed the obvious explanation of the production of a work with so strange an ending was that the poet himself, allowing the subject to get out of hand, could not arrive at a satisfactory answer and yet did not wish to suppress the work.[30]

Later, in the B-text (1376-77?) the writer took up the question with renewed energy and greater confidence where he despairingly broke off in the A-text, deciding there were certain things beyond man's understanding. But Langland's ultimate decision favored the good heathen, for he finally conceded in the C-text (1392-93 or 1398-99) that simple faith must save even the "Saresyns":

'For Saresyns mowe be saued so   yf thei so by-leyuede,
In the lengthynge of here lyf   to leyue on holychurche.'
                                    (*PP*, C, xviii, 123-24)

Juliana of Norwich, too, was keenly aware of the difficulty. On the one hand she clung steadfastly to an orthodox profession of faith:

Our faith is grounded in Gods word, and it longeth to our faith, that we believe that Gods word shall be saved in all thing: and one point of our faith is, that many creatures shall be damned, as angels that fell out of heaven for pride, which be now fiends; and many in earth that dyeth out of the faith of Holy Church; that is to say, those that be heathen: and also many that hath received Christendome, and liveth unchristen life, and so dyeth out of charity; all these shall be damned to hell without end, as Holy Church teacheth me to believe. . . .[31]

On the other hand, Juliana could not but believe that God would keep His promise when He said to her in a vision: 'That, that is unpossible to thee, is not unpossible to mee; I shall save my word in all thing, and I shall make all thing well.'[32] No good man could be damned in a world to which God had given His word that all things should be made well, reasoned Juliana,

[68]

and she dared to assert that all should be saved, since God made all and loved all He made.

For in mankind that shall be saved, is comprehended all; that is to say, all that is made, and the Maker of all; for in man is God, and in God is all; and he that loveth thus, he loveth all.[33]

Juliana's inconsistency, her wavering between belief in damnation and rejection of it, reflects the confusion of the age over these perplexing matters.

There were some troubled souls who could not accept Juliana's solution. In 1347 a certain man of Toulouse, called Peter, was accused of heresy for holding that a loving Creator could not sentence all but a few of his creatures to eternal torment. "This man Peter said also that, if he could hold that God who, of a thousand men whom he had made, saved one and damned all the rest, then he would tear and rend him with tooth and nail as a traitor, and would brand him as false and traitorous, and would spit in his face."[34] Coulton looked to the mystics as the progenitors of this attitude:

The wave of popular mysticism which seems to have begun in Dominican circles on the upper Rhine at the end of the thirteenth century, and thence to have spread by the trade route to the lower Rhine and England, showed, among other manifestations, a strong tendency to escape from the cruel theology which, as very commonly preached and understood, is set forth without exaggeration in this man Peter's words. This humanitarian effort is noticeable in three of Chaucer's contemporaries, Rulman Merswin of Strassburg, Juliana the anchoress of Norwich, and the author (or authors) of *Piers Plowman*.[35]

It is interesting to find a similar tolerance in a man who differed so radically from the mystics as the shrewd and cynical author of *Mandeville's Travels*. He, too, regarded the righteous heathen with a broad-minded sympathy when he said of the people of Synople, who had asked Alexander not for riches but for everlasting life:

I believe that God loveth their service to gree, as he did of Job that was a Paynim, the which he held for his true servant

[69]

and many other. I beeleve well that God loveth al those that love him and serve him mekely and truely, and that despise the vaine glory of the world as these men doe, and as Job did.[36]

The revolt against the horror of eternal judgment culminated in an extensive treatment of the Trajan legend, which Coulton believes was invented to soften the doctrine that all non-Christians were damned.[37] The story of the virtuous pagan ruler, saved by the prayers of Gregory, became the test case of a number of medieval people who believed that a heathen might win salvation through good deeds. Here, too, Thomas Aquinas was the authority. In connection with his discussion of prayer and predestination, Thomas Aquinas had repeatedly referred to Gregory's intercession for Trajan.

Gregory prayed for Trajan, and freed him from hell, as Damascenus tells in a certain dialogue on the dead; and thus it seems that he was freed from the company of reprobates by the prayers of Gregory. . . . Though Trajan was in the place of the reprobates, nevertheless he was not absolutely reprobate, for it was predestined that he be saved by Gregory's prayers.[38]

St. Thomas's case for the salvation of the virtuous heathen on the basis of predestination was eagerly seized upon by fourteenth-century writers as a happy solution. We find Trajan's story appealing alike to men of great minds, like Dante, and to mystics, like Langland; and toward the end of the century a new version appears in England.

About 1386, an unknown writer (variously identified as a West Country man in London or perhaps the *Gawain* poet) wrote an alliterative poem about St. Erkenwald, Saxon Bishop of London, the fourth in succession after St. Augustine, who saved from hell a righteous judge of ancient pagan days.

When St. Paul's Cathedral, once a heathen temple, was being rebuilt, a richly ornate tomb was discovered. Hundreds came to look at it, and marveled. After morning prayers, before a large assembly Bishop Erkenwald had the sepulcher opened, and in it was a perfectly preserved body. The bishop commanded the corpse to tell who he was and why he lay there, and the dead

[70]

man, regaining speech, told how he had for forty years served faithfully and honestly as justice under the pagan ruler, King Belin. But because he was a pagan he was condemned to Limbo. The bishop wept for pity, and his tears, falling upon the good pagan, anointed him, whose soul at once was transported to the land of the blessed.

The story, dignified and elevated into what John Edwin Wells calls "one of the best of the legends in England," corresponds closely to the Trajan legend. It further indicates how vitally important to the Middle Ages was the fate of the righteous heathen, because men—like men of all time—wanted assurance of a benevolent God.

Apparently there were some who went so far as to reject the idea of hell altogether. A Wyclifite tract complained:

. . . many men wenen that ther is no helle of everelastynge peyne, but that God doith but threten us, and not to don it in dede—as is pleyinge of myraclis in sygne, and not in dede.[39]

Some critics of the doctrine were even bolder than those whom this tract described. An anonymous author of a four-teenth-century work intended as a kind of preachers' manual—which had many readers, if we may judge by the great number of manuscripts that have survived—tells a story of arrogant unbelief: A religious man preached a sermon on hell, and a hearer, unwilling to be persuaded, cried: "Woe be to him who believes you! You have never been there!"[40]

Even the immortality of the soul was doubted by some of the worldly-wise, as John Gower records. The poet, Chaucer's friend and contemporary, throughout his voluminous produc-tion of almost a hundred thousand lines in French, Latin, and English, maintains a didactic tone, though his work always shows marked literary skill. If we can believe him, his observa-tions are not so much original as representative of the current views,[41] and the *Mirour de l'omme* reflects general topics of conversation:

> I do not know why I should preach
> To such merchants about the other joy
> Or otherwise about sorrow;

For well they know, he who increases
His wealth in this life
At least has honor of the body:
One of whom said to me, the other day,
That he who can have the sweetness
Of this life and rejects it,
To his mind would act foolishly,
Since, after this life, no one knows the truth,
Whither to go or by what way.[42]

Another layman, a correspondent and admirer of Chaucer's, was Eustache Deschamps (1346-1406), and he too deplored the loss of faith in an after life. As royal messenger of Charles V about 1367 and as holder of other important offices under the king, Deschamps had occasion to travel extensively. He had seen with his own eyes the many horrors inflicted by the wars and was himself a victim of the widespread destruction when his own home was burned by the English army. Embittered by personal misfortune and grieved by the miseries that war had imposed upon France, he poured forth in his verses a hopeless disillusionment in the times. His picture of war, lacking the glamour, excitement, and colorful chivalry of Froissart, is harshly critical but forceful and realistic. Rhetoric, extreme piety, pessimism, and exaggeration there may be; but some basis for the genuine despair of the man surely existed. An output which is more voluminous than inspired, his works are significant not only for the vivid picture of contemporary life but for the fact that the poet represents the orthodox opinion of a layman. He is not a preacher dedicated to winning souls for the glory of God; he is a man of the world, distressed by the reckless living of his fellows, and making an insistent complaint filled with sincere emotion.

Of the many volumes of Deschamps's poems, a considerable number are devoted to lamentations inspired by the corruption which was undermining the spiritual well-being of his countrymen. He often deplored the prevailing lack of faith in a future life. Sweeping assertions rule his verse—"On ne croit plus à rien" becomes a refrain:

Alas! God, what a time and what a mode of life
Runs today throughout the world in general,
Where I do not see a true heart, pure thought,
Pity, love or sure judgment
Keeping the law, making one's salvation,
Honoring God or fearing his power!
But I see the persistence of all evils
In mortal bodies, in always coveting
False honors, rank, and subsistence,
Because Hell and Heaven do not matter to anyone.[43]

This general failure to consider one's soul called forth many of the poet's most earnest lines. There is repetition of the mournful theme: "On ne craint plus ni paradis ni enfer."

Speak who will, instruct who knows how,
Blame the evils, exalt the virtues,
Set forth exempla each such as he can
Of those who are through sins destroyed,
Some drowned and the others hanged,
Of the wrath of God, tempest, famine,
Death, war, torment, hate,
Of the great sufferings that Lucifer will cause;
To show all this is not worth a thorn:
No one fears God, Heaven, or Hell.[44]

This indifference to the after life was most closely associated with the Epicureans of Italy. That this sect exercised a strong influence on Italian minds Dante leaves no shadow of doubt. To Epicurus and "all his followers, Who with the body make the spirit die" he shows no mercy. Along with the notorious Frederick, Dante consigns Farinata, Cavalcante, Cardinal Ubaldini, and "more than a thousand" others to the fiery city of Dis.

It is Dante's freedom in discussing his predecessors and contemporaries, and his frank appraisal of them, that make the *Divine Comedy* invaluable here as an index of his period. Dante had been steeped in learning from early boyhood, so that when he came to write his great masterpiece, an intellectual as well as spiritual monument, he knew what he was about; nothing appears there without purpose, a sense of right and order. So his evaluation of men and events is worth noting as a commentary on the times.

When Dante placed the Epicureans in the sixth circle of the *Inferno,* he had in mind no thought of the Greek school of philosophy—as his commentator Benvenuto da Imola reminds us—but of medieval Christians who had fallen from grace by the sin of infidelity. Clearly, the poet had compassion for those who, born before the Christian era or in an unchristian land, had no opportunity to become Christians but had attained renown for scientific or intellectual achievement. But to Dante the worst sinner was the one who denied his faith, his deadliest sin the negation of immortality. "And by way of preface I say that of all stupidities that is the most foolish, the basest, and the most pernicious, which believes that after this life there is no other. . . ." (*Conv.,* Tr. II, ix) It was the heresy for which he created the most agonizing punishment—the punishment held by the Church to be the just fate of the unbeliever: death by fire. While looking upon the flaming sepulchers of the heretics, the poet suffers his most terrifying experience. Not only is he anguished at sight of the tortured bodies of the condemned, but troubled about their souls which had been hardened by despair and unbelief.

For Farinata degli Uberti, Dante might have had a fellow feeling, since Farinata was a Ghibelline and in 1260 was the only man with the courage to cast the dissenting vote that would stay the utter destruction of the poet's beloved Florence. But Farinata, though a wise and honorable man, had openly confessed, as an imitator of Epicurus, according to Benvenuto, that he refused to believe there was any other world than this, whence he constantly was striving to excel in this short life because he did not expect another that would be better.[45] Dante could not overlook such bold heresy and was constrained to leave a fellow Florentine in eternal infamy. The poet depicts him as a man of all the fierce pride, hardness, and absorbing selfishness associated with the Epicureans. It is Farinata himself who, in the *Inferno,* testifies to the great number of "outcasts of Heaven, race despised," who keep him company: "With

[74]

more than a thousand lie I here; the second Frederick is here within, and the Cardinal; and of the rest I speak not." (*Inf.,* X)

Cavalcante Cavalcanti's presence in the *Inferno* signifies Dante's impartial judgment of good and evil, for Cavalcante was the father of Guido, formerly one of Dante's dearest friends. The breaking of the bond between the two, who for their close friendship have been called David and Jonathan, marks one of the tragedies of the poet's life. The cause of their estrangement is not known; perhaps the son had been influenced by his father's heretical thought;[46] or, as a philosopher, he scorned poetry; or favored vulgar poets above the Latin;[47] or through the years for one reason or another found less in common with his boyhood friend. In any case, it was Dante's hard duty, as one of the official Priori of Florence, to banish his friend to Sarazana, where he caught a fever which caused his death in 1306. Whatever the relationship of the two younger men, Dante could not on account of personal feeling fail to punish any transgressors of the law of Holy Church. So we find him condemning even Cavalcante, his closest friend's father, for Cavalcante was an Epicurean, as Benvenuto testifies when he declares that the man had wholly defended the Epicurean sect, always believing, and persuading others to believe, that the soul died with the body.[48]

Not unexpectedly, Dante meted out to Cardinal Ubaldini the hardest fate he could devise, because here was a man who represented the worst possible moral lapse, since a churchman who violated the high purpose of his calling was an offender against both God and man. Repeatedly Dante points out that the whole trouble with the Church is the lust of its leaders for power and wealth. So he deals sternly with the Cardinal who frankly admitted materialism as well as doubt, who was reported to have declared: "If I have a soul, I have lost it a thousand times for the Ghibellines."[49]

Dante's criticism of the materialistic thought which resulted in immoral and unchristian living, in Epicureanism, and in profession of infidelity, is well known. Canto X of the *Inferno* in its entirety lays a heavy charge against unbelievers.

[75]

The poet had already indicated in Canto IX the extent of current skepticism and its potential danger to the spiritual well-being of the faithful. Virgil, symbolizing higher wisdom, is moved to protect Dante from Gorgon—representing unbelief—by preventing him from looking into the perilous depth of doubt. That is, even to the most faithful, contemplation of evil may prove fatal to the soul except for aid from a higher power. This is why Epicureanism was looked upon as so great a threat to society. This is why Dante was so deeply troubled by Farinata's declaration that the Sadducees numbered more than a thousand. Benvenuto explains that the poet declined to name them because "It would take too long to enumerate the eminent men of the Epicurean sect. . . . Ah, how many heretics there are who seem Catholics hypocritically for fear of punishment or infamy!"[50]

Francesco Sacchetti was likewise disturbed by the skepticism of fatalistic philosophers. Sacchetti (c. 1335-1400) was a man of mediocre but charming talents, representative of late fourteenth-century Italy which he pictured vividly in tales of bourgeois life. But he likewise wrote sermons, *I Sermoni Evangelici,* and it is these which are of interest here, for Sacchetti, commenting on Scripture and illustrating his points with homely anecdotes and examples of men he knew, reveals a good many popular ideas. In his sermon on humility, he points a sternly reproving finger at the fatalistic philosophers who refused to see the divine hand in any phase of life and who therefore deemed fate a matter of an irrevocable and predestined plan, irrespective of good or evil living.

There was one group of philosophers who said that in this life nature produces all things through necessity, as it was ordained from the beginning of the world, and that it was of no avail to preach and pray, because in the beginning everything was placed where it was destined to remain.[51]

Loss of faith in supplication for divine help and guidance was a matter of concern to the Church: the clergy reprimanded the folk who did not know their prayers;[52] they taught that it was

[76]

essential, as Piers the Plowman put it, "to percen with a pater-noster the paleys of heuene." H. S. Bennett found evidence that the clergy of the Middle Ages insisted on the necessity of prayer, which "was not merely a means of asking for God's help, but was in itself a spiritual grace."[53] Resignation that left no place for prayer was a natural result of the spiritual con-flict inherent in the problem of determinism. It was the kind of fatalism attributed to the Epicureans. And like his more illustrious predecessor Dante, Sacchetti had much to say about this sect "who held, with much vain reasoning, that once the body is dead the soul is dead."[54]

Heresy also took the form of doubting the mystery and the efficacy of the Eucharist. So loath were some rationalists to accept the miracle of transubstantiation that many of them de-fied the Church rather than profess what seemed false to their practical knowledge and in their daily experience. Walsingham describes one such skeptic who said "clearly it is not the body of Christ which is handled sacramentally in the Church, but some inanimate thing worse than a toad or spider, which are live animals."[55] This heretic was repeatedly urged to recant but, unwilling to give up his opinion, he died at the stake. People feel deeply who pay so dearly.

Preachers of the time, troubled by this general indifference to the sacrament, denounced the practical attitude of the man in the street. The author of Le Mireour du monde took him to task for his refusal to believe unquestioningly in revealed truth: "Therefore, because he cannot understand or see how a whole man can be in that wafer which the priest holds at the altar, he will not believe that it is truly the body of God."[56]

When dogmas and the sacraments were rejected it was often on the basis of materialistic reasoning; to those practical souls without great faith, all that they accepted must be capable of proof. What was apparent to these and demonstrated daily was the injustice in the distribution of good and evil.

Sacchetti described the belief, frequently held among the folk, that men were at the mercy of an irrational force which, arbitrarily and without regard for personal merit, dealt out good and evil. "Ignorant people—those who think our bodies like those of irrational animals—believe that in this life there are many good people who will always have persecution and misfortune, and many wicked people who will always receive good things."[57] Fatalism was the popular answer to the question of good and evil. It was a philosophy of despair, and there is evidence that it had to some extent infected both the common people and the upper class.

It was not unusual to hear the lords complain bitterly of God's wisdom. Langland, shocked by man's refusal to accept the divine will in all things, describes the arguments commonly heard at the tables of the rich:

> I haue yherde hiegh men   etyng atte table,
> Carpen as thei clerkes were   of Cryste and of his migtes,
> And leyden fautes vppon the fader   that fourmed vs alle,
> And carpen ayeine clerkes   crabbed wordes;—
>
> (*PP*, B, x, 101-104)

Like many another who has failed to find a philosophical answer to the problem of evil, fourteenth-century men helplessly shifted the responsibility to the God who made them. If He were all-powerful, as the priests declared, then how came the Devil by so much success?

> "Whi wolde owre saueoure suffre   suche a worme in his blisse,
> That bigyled the womman   and man after,
> Thorw whiche wyles and wordes   thei wenten to helle,
> And al her sede for here synne   the same deth suffred?"
>
> (*PP*, B, x, 105-108)

The question has perplexed the profoundest minds. Ultimately, the man who cannot accept mystery on faith must end by reasoning stubbornly that what is not sensible is therefore false:

> "Whi shulde we that now ben   for the werkes of Adam
> Roten and to-rende?   resoun wolde it neuere."
>
> (*PP*, B, x, 111-12)

It is the conclusion that comes naturally to a mind that rationalizes the meaning of life on the basis of human experience.

[78]

No less grieved than Langland but far more hopeful is Juliana in her consideration of the problem of good and evil. Despite a life of seclusion and solitude, Juliana had a curiously keen insight into the problems of men, for whom she had infinite compassion and understanding. Like them, she was troubled about God's justice, though she never in any sense doubted His goodness or lost faith that all would be well. In her meditations upon God's dealings with His creatures, she came upon the old problem: if God knew sin would ruin His plan, then why did He permit sin to come into the world? Juliana could not find the answer save in an unfaltering faith that all in due time would be explained. But still she yearned over suffering, sinning mankind and wondered why it suffered and sinned:

. . . I saw nothing letted me but sin. And so I beheld generally in us all; and methought, if sin had not been we should all have been clean and like to our Lord as he made us. And thus in my folly, before this time, often I wondered why, by the great aforesaid wisdom of God, the beginning of sin was not letted, for then thought me that all should have been well. . . . 'Ah good Lord, how might all be well, for the great harm that is to come by sin to thy creatures?'[58]

She was not unaware of the unorthodoxy of her belief that all sin would be forgiven:

'How may this be? for I know by the common teaching of Holy Church, and by mine own feeling, that the blame of our sins continually hangeth upon us fro the first man, into the time that we come up into heaven.'[59]

But "when the doome is given, and we be all brought up above, then shall we clearly see in God the privities which now be hid to us. And then shall none of us be stirred to say in any thing, 'Lord, if it had been thus, it had been well.' "[60]

Juliana had a human heart and a mind that was sometimes given to doubts; but she attained serenity both by an acceptance of things as they are and by a glowing faith in the things to be. It is her gentleness in dealing with mortal sin that makes her

[79]

plea for mankind outstanding. Throughout her inspired pages one catches refreshing glimpses of a clean and shining world, strangely contrasting with that of many contemporary religious who declared that unless men repented of sin, there was imminent danger they would plunge into an eternity of darkness and terror. Few saw such bright hope as came to Juliana in her revelations.

Skepticism took many forms of expression in the fourteenth century. There is the doubt and questioning of a confused or simple mind; the bitter rejection of faith by a poor and oppressed common people; the scoffing attitude of the reckless rich, content enough with this world and indifferent to the next; the open hypocrisy of a corrupt clergy; the frank disbelief of the faithless. There was also in non-religious literature the passing commentary, which indicates, more clearly than all the pointed condemnations and criticisms of God's justice, that skeptical ideas were abroad and had become part of casual conversation. An interesting example of this kind of evidence appears in Froissart's *Chronicles*.

Jean Froissart, whose work is closely bound up with historical events of fourteenth-century England, was a native of the province of Hainault, who wrote in French, and lived most of his life in his own country. Yet there is good reason to include his name in English historical and literary records. For eight years a confidant of Queen Philippa (1361-69), companion to Prince Lionel at the time of the latter's marriage, again a visitor to the Isles in 1395, Froissart was on intimate terms with persons of the English court. More important to this study is his interest in a careful and accurate record of all he learned about the people of England. He had the art of making people tell him everything they knew; and the many facts thus gained from personal contact he methodically set down in his notebook. His work is a vivid, colorful, uncritical account of his impressions. He made no attempt to philosophize or interpret events but he described in great detail exactly what he heard and saw.

In 1395 Froissart was a guest of Richard II, to whom he

[80]

presented a book that "treated matters of love" and which, according to the not too modest author, pleased the English king greatly. A squire, Henry Christead, having seen the book, struck up an acquaintance with the Frenchman. Knowing Froissart's reputation as a historian, Christead—with the expressed intention that the writer might put the story "in perpetual memory"—told of Richard's conquest in Ireland. Christead described Ireland as one of the most evil countries of the world to make war on because of its wild and inhospitable terrain, the savagery of its soldiers, the rudeness of its people. Yet when Richard entered the country, heralded by the Earl of Ormond, Ireland's four most powerful kings promptly submitted themselves to Richard at Dublin and offered obedience to the crown of England, "by the grace of God."

Froissart listened attentively to Christead's story, but we can almost see the quizzical smile with which he heard the climax. He was frankly skeptical of the narrator's attribution of the extraordinary victory to divine power:

But one thynge I wolde desyre of you to knowe, howe these four kynges of Irelande came so soone to the kynge of Englandes obeysaunce, whan kynge Edwarde the kynges graunfather, who was so valyaunt a prince and so redouted over all, coude never subdue them nor putte them under, and yet he had alwayes warre with them, and in that they are subdued nowe, ye sayd it was by treatie, and by the grace of God. Indede the grace of God is good, who so can have it, it is moche worthe; but it is sene nowe a dayes, that erthely princes getteth lytell without it be by puissaunce.[61]

Froissart could not have been greatly surprised at Christead's admission that in addition to God's grace, the English king had also on his side an army of such numbers and wealth as "abashed the Irishmen!"

Worldliness was an outstanding characteristic of Froissart and it gave his viewpoint a secular tone unexpected in a canon of the Church. When an ecclesiastic could declare that according to his observation the favor of God counted for little unless backed by force, we can see how far even a man in holy orders in the fourteenth century had moved away from a rigid belief in the absolute power and justice of God.

This religious criticism in the fourteenth century was not new, for it dated back to the thirteenth century, as we have seen, and before. But the later period is of greater interest to literature because more and more the written word discloses not only the ecclesiastical but the literary mind; we begin to see more of the imaginative genius and less of the theological, more of the life of the people and less of its soul. Increased interest in the people, from the viewpoint of the secular writers, like Langland, Deschamps, "Mandeville," Chaucer, Boccaccio, and others, resulted in a literary production that helps reveal the popular mind.

That the popular mind was not so submissive and uncritical as has been supposed is apparent in the literature, in which a surprising number throughout Christendom expressed considerable freedom of thought, questioned dogmas, the doctrine of immortality, the efficacy of the sacraments, the justice of divine will, and the very existence of God. The times seemed to provoke a state of mind which Coulton said was "as definitely sceptical as the scepticism of the eighteenth century or of our own day."[62] MacCulloch observed this mingling of moral and spiritual and philosophical issues: "The spirit of revolt against the Church was now religious, now irreligious, and against specific beliefs or against creed and cult as a whole. But the two were apt to intermingle. The demands of the Church on mind and conscience tended to overreach themselves; and especially in men of wealth and power, able to indulge their passions freely, they produced indifference to religion, unbelief going hand in hand with immorality and materialism."[63] It is this skepticism that I have tried to show, together with reference to moral and social conditions that may have contributed to its spread. And I have drawn chiefly upon primary sources in order to let the medieval people speak for themselves.

The general conclusion is not far from that of Mary Morton Wood, who has extensively illustrated the spirit of protest characterizing medieval life and thought: Whatever we moderns are prone to call the Middle Ages, "Contemporary writers did not regard their own age as an age of faith."[64]

4.   Chaucer

THERE WERE MANY OUTWARD SIGNS OF RELIGION IN CHAUCER'S England, an essentially Catholic England—the impressive cathedrals, the stained glass, the wall paintings, the sculpture, the holy shrines, the wayside crosses, the relics. Yet it is made clear in fourteenth-century literature that if the majority of people were believers, there were not a few whose "studie was but litel on the Bible." These dared question the state of affairs into which they had been born, expressing perplexity about the heaven they had been taught to hope for, the hell they had learned to fear; rationalizing the sacraments they had grown up to reverence; exercising their minds over problems of determinism and man's free will which baffled even the churchmen; protesting against a sea of troubles by opposing God's justice —or injustice—with common sense.

It will be shown, later, in what ways Chaucer displayed an awareness of these ideas. That he was interested in them is apparent in his own work; *why* he was interested becomes equally clear after a consideration of his life, his particular type of inquiring mind and complex nature, his vocation that took him into a world of men and his avocation that took him into a realm of books. Even if we find no proof that Chaucer himself held a skeptical view, there is every evidence that he was well aware of those aspects of skepticism pointed out in previous chapters on the thirteenth and fourteenth centuries. Not only in his own discussion of controversial matters but in his dramatic presentation of them through the characters in his stories he puts forth his views cogently and coherently in a way that contemporary readers would understand.

It is not surprising if Chaucer, "the mirror of his age," reflected some of the ideas that were current among all classes of people in his day. A lifetime of experience in the service of his king, at home and abroad, during an interesting, tempestuous, changing period of medieval history, had brought before Chaucer's observant eyes a vivid panorama, and to his ears the talk of the time. No man of his period had a better chance to know what was going on around him, for his many offices—as page, squire, ambassador, customs controller, clerk, forester, soldier—had given him broad contacts.

In the execution of duties that kept him in the midst of the extravagant courts of Edward III and Richard II, Chaucer mingled with distinguished men and women, including kings and queens and knights, diplomats and scholars, men of law and men of letters. Such contacts were not confined to his own country but extended also to Italy and France, where he was sent on the king's business. Furthermore, Chaucer, son of a prosperous wine merchant, was well acquainted with the class of people from whom he himself came and with whom he constantly dealt. He often had business with merchants, tradespeople, craftsmen, shopkeepers, vintners, clerks, and various officeholders.

Moreover, with his interest in people, he was a man to make the most of his opportunities. Certainly anyone who claims to have observed at an inn the "sondry folk" who entered there, and before sundown of a certain day in April to have met some twenty-nine travelers and "spoken with hem everichon," was a good mixer. The Canterbury pilgrims, diverse and vivid as they are, themselves suggest the kinds and number of people Chaucer knew. For these sundry folk represent not just fourteenth-century types, but a number of distinct individuals. J. M. Manly has rightly pointed out that "behind his most vital and successful sketches lay the observation of living men and women."[1] If there were skeptical notions in the air, we may be sure that Chaucer heard about them.

A successful officeholder, a man among men, who somehow found time to produce an impressive volume of writings, not in an ivory tower but in the midst of activities of a thriving city, Chaucer has well been called a product of the fourteenth-century world of affairs. It is easy to understand how he became the mirror of his age.

Obviously Chaucer's knowledge of the world of men and ideas came to him firsthand through his official duties and his wide acquaintance, but he knew them also through his broad range of reading. If he heard among the people he knew expressions of skepticism that aroused his interest, such ideas as came to his mind could have been further stimulated by what he read. We have his own word for it that he was an insatiable reader and in leisure hours could seldom be lured away from his books by other delights. Lounsbury has enumerated the great number of works that were known to Chaucer, sometimes in the original, sometimes in translation.[2] This is not to say that he was a profound scholar. He himself repeatedly disclaimed any credit as a learned man. Like the Parson, he would modestly have invited correction for not being "textueel"—and rightly, because, as Lounsbury showed, his knowledge was neither deep nor altogether accurate. But his easy familiarity with world literature would today belong only to a man of learning and education. An eager mind led him into many fields, and his constant allusion to literary, philosophical, and scientific works suggests how widely—even if sometimes superficially—he read in ancient as well as medieval writings, in French, Italian, and Latin as well as in English.

One of his favorite books was the *Roman de la Rose,* which influenced him all his life. He had a command of the Latin writers—Virgil, Seneca, Macrobius, Statius, Lucan, Claudian, Livy; Ovid he claimed as his "oune bok"; and Boethius probably helped shape most of his philosophical thought. He knew of Homer, Aristotle, and Plato through later Latin poets and writers. Most of Aristotle's work and many commentaries on it had for some time been available in Latin; though Chaucer may never have read Aristotle, he must have heard a good deal about him. He was familiar with the writings of the Church Fathers, with Bradwardine and Bernardus Silvestris, with the Golden Legend and the legends of the saints. He knew of the Matter of Britain, France, and Rome; he knew the great

[86]

volume of literature on the Trojan wars. He had some knowledge of medicine, mathematics, astronomy and astrology, and
theories of sound and motion, even though much of what he
knew about science Professor Pauline Aiken has shown[3] came
from the encyclopaedia of Vincent of Beauvais. Conscious artist
that he was, he had studied the technique of rhetoric: though
in later years he derided Geoffrey de Vinsauf, author of *Poetria
Nova* (*c.* 1200), he acknowledged the rhetorician as his "deere
maister soverayn" whom he followed in his early work. He
certainly knew many works of fourteenth-century writers, in
England as elsewhere: in France, notably those of Deschamps,
Machaut, Froissart; in Italy, especially those of Dante, Boccaccio, and Petrarch "the lauriat poete" who "Enlumyned al Ytaille
of poetrie." Considering the limited leisure that his burden of
daily work must have allowed him, we find that even a sam-
pling of the books Chaucer knew best forms an impressive list.

From the books he read, it is easy to see that Chaucer was
more than ordinarily endowed with intellectual curiosity. Much
of his reading indicates his robust interest not only in the world
of men but the world of ideas—scientific, philosophical, and
ethical. This interest, which we find often in his works, helps
explain why he might naturally have been alert to any skeptical
ideas that were circulating by word of mouth or in the written
page.

There is his interest in dreams that is almost always present
in the early works and which continued intermittently throughout his life. This interest manifested itself not as mere fancy
that appealed to his poetic imagination or as a convenient
literary device so popular with the French masters whose influence is prominent in the *Book of the Duchess,* the *Parliament
of Fowls,* and the *Legend of Good Women,* but as a complex
medieval doctrine. If the discussion in the *House of Fame* is
hardly a serious one, the sixty-five lines of the first book describing the causes, significance, and fulfillment of dreams reveal a matter much discussed by medieval men and women.
Though he might profess abysmal ignorance on the subject,
Chaucer was apparently familiar with the best known theories.

[87]

In his discourse on dreams in the *House of Fame* he was chiefly indebted to the *Roman de la Rose,* though he seems also to have drawn upon Macrobius, who in the fifth century in his Commentary on Cicero's *Somnium Scipionis* had preserved a fragment of the *De Re Publica.* In the *Nun's Priest's Tale* the doctrine of dreams becomes a subject of lively debate between the learned cock Chauntecleer and his skeptical mate Pertelote. Here, too, Chaucer uses Macrobius, to whom Chauntecleer refers as an authority on the belief that dreams serve as "Warnynge of thynges that men after seen." Though the cock is the "intellectual," it is Pertelote who takes the side of contemporary learned opinion, scoffing at her husband's belief in the prophetic significance of the dream experience—much like the worldly-wise Pandarus, who dismissed it as not worth a bean. As in the *House of Fame,* it is suggested that certain kinds of dreams may be attributed to physical origin, and Pertelote's practical diagnosis of the uneasy Chauntecleer's "malencolie" and her prescription of a "laxatyf" to cure his disorder are in accord with general medical practice and indicate Chaucer's familiarity with it.

It is possible, since the literature Chaucer knew abounds in dream lore, that he was consciously utilizing also in such discussions the theories of writers like John of Salisbury, Vincent of Beauvais, Bartholomaeus Anglicus, Robert Holkot, the astrologer Haly, and Arnoldus de Villa Nova. Professor Curry declares that he "cannot imagine Chaucer's having been ignorant of these universally accepted conclusions; he might have had access to most of the authors . . . any one of whom—Vincent de Beauvais, for example—might have given him the general trend of opinion."[4]

A more serious matter than dream lore that aroused Chaucer's interest, and one of importance to all thinking men of the Middle Ages, was the question of predestination. Chaucer had available a volume of writings on the subject, but his chief authority was the *Consolation of Philosophy* of Boethius, who in the form of a dialogue between himself and Lady Philosophy sets forth the problem of free will and predestination. The writer states certain problems that we find also in Chaucer. Is there free will or does destiny rule men's actions and deeds? (V, Pr. 2) Why pray to God if He has already predestined what men desire? (V, Pr. 3) Do things happen because God foreordains them or does God foresee them because they are going to happen? (V, Pr. 3) It is evident that Chaucer's interest in such questions persisted, for he more than once refers to the doctrine of predestination and—at least in two instances, *Troilus and Criseyde* and the *Nun's Priest's Tale*—engages in somewhat detailed discussions.

That Chaucer had heard endless arguments on the subject of free will is suggested by the Nun's Priest's assertion that it had been a matter of dispute by "an hundred thousand men"! (*NPT,* 3239) Little wonder that Chaucer was concerned about a question so provocative in his day. His debt to Boethius in forming his own opinion has been fully discussed by Bernard L. Jefferson, who traced the influence of the *Consolation* from *Troilus* through the *Canterbury Tales.*[5] This writer points out how deeply the poet himself had thought about the subject, always basing his discussions on the *Consolation,* but not accepting its conclusions.

That Chaucer should have his characters persistently assume this attitude perhaps bespeaks his own point of view. . . . If the question of free will remains an open one in his mind, he is unique among the mediaeval writers who discussed this subject, and who might have had some weight with him. Boethius, Bradwardine, St. Augustine, Jean de Meun, and Dante all took sides one way or another on the problem.[6]

Another subject which won Chaucer's attention was the doctrine of *gentilesse.* There is nothing new or radical in Chaucer's consideration of true nobility as a quality apart from lineage, but it is striking that a man in court circles should dwell upon the subject. The Wife of Bath permits the Loathly Lady to preach a long sermon on gentility, poverty, and age. Since the discourse on gentility has little dramatic probability—if, as is unlikely, such a woman had discussed the subject, she would hardly have had at the tip of her tongue the writings of Dante and Seneca and Boethius—it is certainly Chaucer who speaks here, and speaks volubly.

There is no question that Chaucer had thought about Dante's views on the matter, for he names "the wise poete of Florence." That he had read further on the subject is evident in the Wife's reference to Seneca and Boethius as authorities. Common both to Dante and to Boethius was the idea that true nobility is virtue which comes from God alone, a concept that is strongly emphasized in the ballade *Gentilesse.* In the Wife's tale and the ballade, there is also a marked influence of the *Roman de la Rose.* But Chaucer's conclusions are colored by his personality and characteristic interest in human nature, for to him gentility includes not only godliness and noble ideals but the simple, homely traits of living men and women: a person of *gentilesse* was "Trewe of his word, sobre, pitous, and free, Clene of his gost, and loved besinesse." Lowes observed that in the passages on *gentilesse* "the fine democracy of Jean de Meun's conception of true nobility has been merged with Dante's loftier idealism, and both have been tempered by Chaucer's own broad humanity."[7]

We can see another evidence of Chaucer's intellectual curiosity in his translations of works which involved current controversies. Boethius had made a greater impression on medieval writers than any other philosopher except Aristotle. Chaucer naturally knew the *Consolation of Philosophy.* That he undertook the task of putting it into Middle English (about 1380) indicates what vital interest it had for the poet. Perhaps no single work he knew discussed so many philosophical problems that stimulated his mind. Free will and predestination, fortune, providence, God's justice and the problem of evil, true nobility, power, fame, wealth, destiny, and truth are some of the subjects about which Boethius had posed philosophical questions, and all may be found in Chaucer's work.

Such problems as these he considered, too, in another work that he translated. Whether or not Chaucer translated all or part of the *Roman de la Rose,* it was a work he knew well in its entirety. There survives only a fragment of the Middle

English translation which can be confidently attributed to Chaucer—and that, the graceful idealization of courtly love by Guillaume de Lorris. But the poet himself implies that he has translated a portion at least of the cynical work by Jean de Meun, who covers a variety of topics: science, philosophy, love, youth, old age, women, society, theology. The translation is dated early in Chaucer's career, and the continued influence of Jean de Meun is evident in many ideas and even specific lines found in later works.

If less conducive to controversy than his other translations, Chaucer's *Tale of Melibee,* closely following the French original *Livre de Melibée et de Dame Prudence,* displays his interest in current moral and ethical ideas. Included in the *Canterbury Tales,* it is generally assigned to the poet's later period.[8] Though today it seems tedious reading, it apparently held the attention of the fourteenth century, for the usually outspoken Canterbury pilgrims heard it out to the finish, and the Host loudly praised the patient Dame Prudence, whose example he would have his own shrewish wife follow. Since the poet went to the trouble of translating the prose work, he must have had more than passing interest in a "moral tale vertuous" which treated in detail the ideals of prudence, courage, wisdom, patience, tolerance, forgiveness, justice, reason, discretion, and peace.

These are only a few of the subjects which held Chaucer's sustained interest and which reveal the intellectual curiosity that was characteristic of the poet throughout his life. If among these problems which concerned his contemporaries there was speculation about doctrine, if there was wavering between faith and doubt, if there was skepticism as well as faith among the people he knew, then Chaucer was often exposed to liberal and rationalistic thought. What were his reactions to these problems?

Properly to appraise Chaucer's attitudes, to determine what his own convictions were, is not easy. Such an appraisal is the more difficult because Chaucer was sometimes subtle in his humor; he was given to changing moods; he seemed capable of entertaining different points of view; he was endowed with a many-sided genius. And all of these traits of the man and the poet must be considered in estimating his work.

Chaucer's humor often depends upon his rare gift for irony and satire, and it is not always possible to know whether the poet was writing seriously or in jest. Irony and mockery contribute to difficulties of interpretation. Humor may be taken too seriously (*KnT,* 1785) and irony as sincere conviction (*MerT,* 1267 *ff.*): Theseus's flippant words on love addressed to Palamon and Arcite, delightfully human and amusing, have led to the suggestion that the poet intended a serious attack on courtly love;[9] while the Merchant's praise of marriage, generally recognized as bitterly ironical, has been called by an early scholar a "eulogy of matrimonial bliss,"[10] and, by another, the poet's "perception of a sacred bond, spiritual and indestructible, in true marriage between man and woman."[11] It is no reflection on our judgment if we do not always read the correct meanings into Chaucer: John Marston—who lived in a period over three hundred years nearer Chaucer's than our own —wrote in 1598: "*Chaucer* is harde euen to our vnderstandings; who knows not the reason? Howe much more those old Satyres which expresse themselues in termes, that breathed not long euen in their daies."[12]

Then there is the matter of Chaucer's different moods which also add to difficulties of interpretation and necessitate the reader's deciding in what vein the poet was writing. He could be fanciful in the *Book of the Duchess,* realistic in the *Miller's Tale,* amusing in the *Nun's Priest's Tale,* tender in the *Prioress's Tale,* pessimistic in *Troilus and Criseyde,* sentimental in the *Clerk's Tale,* coarse in the *Reeve's Tale,* moralistic in *Melibee,* playful in *Sir Thopas,* repentant in the *Retractions.* Professor George R. Stewart has suggested that Chaucer was subject to moods that varied from one time to another. At one time, in regard to the deeper problems of life, "he was able to see no solution except through religion"; and at another, he could offer only "a philosophy of life which is pessimistic."[13] He is all the more real to us as a person, the more human, if like most of

[92]

us he had times of depression as well as of joy and optimism, but these moods must be taken into account in a judgment of his intellectual outlook.

Chaucer's many points of view likewise make it difficult for the reader to reach a clear understanding of what he believed. Whether he changed his mind about issues, or was capable of seeing both sides of a question, or vacillated, his presentation of first one view and then another easily lays him open to the charge of inconsistency and contradiction. In the Marriage Group, for example, we have a debate on the question of authority in married life. The Wife of Bath upholds the case for woman's sovereignty, the Clerk for the subjugation of woman to her husband. The Merchant treats the whole subject of matrimony with bitter irony, favoring neither the senile January nor the faithless May. Whether the final work in the group, the *Franklin's Tale,* was presented simply in contrast to the others or intended as a solution of the problem in a happy compromise between husband and wife, the harmonious relationship of Arveragus and Dorigen stands as a condemnation of the domestic infelicity resulting from the attempt to establish either the man's or the woman's authority in marriage. In any case, the poet gives us all the possible arguments, and who can say which expresses his own opinion?

It is also important, in estimating Chaucer's works, to take into consideration the many-sidedness of his genius. Few writers have shown his facility for turning a hand to such a variety of genres: love-vision, chivalric romance, sustained narrative, legend, fabliau, lai, adventure tale, miracle story, allegory, lyric, ballade. It is inevitable that in such diverse writings we should find representatives of all kinds of men and women, no one of whom we can single out and say, "This is Chaucer." For their creator was not any one of them, he was all of them, as Professor Stewart points out—"a little of the Miller, more of the Squire, a bit of the Wife, a touch of the Maunciple, something (not very much I feel) of that strange elvish creature with downcast eyes, most of all probably of the Clerk, and finally no inconsiderable portion of the Parson."[14]

Besides this consideration of Chaucer's mind, mood, and genius, it is likewise well to remember that he was a dramatic artist. Although it is sometimes reasonably clear that he put his own thoughts in the mouths of his characters, often there is no reason to believe that he was not merely a skilled dramatist at work, depicting a man of a certain type in a given situation which by dramatic necessity required him to speak or act as he does. It is a mark of his versatility that Chaucer was able to enter the diverse minds of his characters. Though realism is achieved partly by vivid description of physical appearance, it is largely due to an understanding of human nature and a keen dramatic sense which permitted the poet to put himself in another's place, momentarily to think, speak, and act like him.

There is, for example, the Merchant, whom we know not only by his forked beard and beaver hat and dignified bearing but by his ironic attitude toward women. The keenly observant and widely read Chaucer could not want material for such a character in an age that was not lacking in anti-feminist literature.[15] That the Merchant's acrimonious attitude is not the poet's own we may believe by his other works; but he noted the seamy as well as the blessed side of marriage. The invective against wedlock, so effectively sustained that it is one of the most forceful and satiric arguments in the marriage debate, shows Chaucer's skill and insight when he puts himself in another's place. So successful is he that one critic has regarded it as an indication of anti-feminism—or at least "a balance against the poet's own sentiments of gallantry."[16]

Another case in point is that of the Wife of Bath, a character in whom Chaucer took obvious delight. Hearty, spirited, rather raucously humorous, earthy, and sociable, the Wife is likable, though in no way excused for faults and behavior unbecoming in woman. Her extraordinary harangue upon "virginitee" is so emphatic that it is taken by several scholars as a theme on which the poet himself felt strongly enough to speak out and to express his recognition of "the fallacy of the prevailing ideal of celibacy."[17]

Equally vivid is the Canon's Yeoman, who is uncommonly

bitter in his exposé of his master's cupidity. It has been suggested that Chaucer wrote the tale in a moment of resentment over being himself duped by some sly alchemist.[18] Though there is no reason to believe that the poet's gullibility ever exposed him to such trickery, he was able to put himself in the Yeoman's place and leave on his reader a lasting impression of the irate, confused mind of one of the most realistic pilgrims in the *Canterbury Tales*.

Now if we recognize in Chaucer a dramatic artist and a man of complex nature, with a subtle gift of expression, given to changing moods, capable of entertaining different points of view, we can see the difficulties involved in understanding his thought. These facets of his nature and genius are of special importance in any study of Chaucer's religion.

Opinion as to Chaucer's religion differs widely. Some writers, like Root and Coulton, have accepted him as a good Christian but not an altogether unquestioning one.[19] Others, like Wells and Simon and Maxfield,[20] have asked whether it is possible from indecisive evidence to know whether the noncommittal Chaucer was or was not an orthodox Catholic. A considerable number of scholars, as Professor Roger S. Loomis has indicated in his article "Was Chaucer a Laodicean?" agree that Chaucer did not take a stand on moral, social, and religious issues because of indifference or good-natured acceptance, because of innate optimism or tolerance, because of detachment, prudence, or diplomacy.[21] Extreme views have represented him as a thoroughgoing Wyclifite,[22] and a forerunner of the Reformation.[23] None of these has omitted mention of the critical and even skeptical tendency in Chaucer's general thought, but none has demonstrated that in religion he was an agnostic or an infidel.

Indeed there is reason to believe that Chaucer was in the main a good Catholic. Canon Looten is one of those who have placed Chaucer among the orthodox. "La sincérité de la foi chrétienne de Chaucer, pour nous du moins, est sans l'ombre d'un doute."[24] Looten refutes criticism of Chaucer provoked by his reputation for satire and independent judgment regarding

accepted thought. ". . . s'il attaque telle ou telle personne in-
dividuelle, nulle part il n'incrimine l'Eglise prise en corps. S'il
est mal à l'aise en face de tel ou tel dogme en particulier, nulle
part il ne met en question ni l'ensemble de la révélation chrétienne, ni l'autorité doctrinale qui la maintient et la défend,
ni la compétence des maîtres qui l'enseignent."[25]

J. S. P. Tatlock, too, has given the poet a place among the
orthodox. "We have no reason to doubt that he went to mass
at least on Sundays and holy days, and to confession and com-
munion at least once a year; and that at the hour of death he
would have been disturbed if he had missed absolution, unction,
and the viaticum."[26]

Likewise, John Edwin Wells, who has not overlooked the
skeptical Chaucer and certain advanced attitudes which placed
him at the forefront of his age, cannot but believe that "Apparently, he was quite in accord with the general tenets of the
Church."[27]

Certainly such views are strongly upheld by Chaucer's sympathetic dramatic treatment of faith in the *Canterbury Tales.*
The poet's respect for the Church and its fundamental doctrine
is so inescapably present in his work that few readers can miss
the religious implications of the poet's declaration of faith as
set forth in the speech of his immortal characters. There is the
Man of Law's Tale, probably written early, before the *Canterbury* period, and revised about 1390. It is a popular medieval
story that combines the Calumniated Wife of folklore with
moralizing passages from the *De Contemptu Mundi;* but Chaucer handled his materials freely and expanded them with
philosophical interpolations. Many religious passages are not
in Trivet, the poet's source: Who protected Constance, the poet
asks, in her tragic plight? And the answer is one of simple
faith: "No wight but Crist, sanz faille." How did this frail
woman meet such great adversity? "Wel may men seen, it nas
but Goddes grace." Constance is the ideal Christian lady, em-
bodying the most Christian virtues of humility and faith, whose
"herte is verray chambre of hoolynesse."

In the *Second Nun's Tale,* another early work, written

perhaps shortly after 1373, Chaucer adapts the legend of St. Cecilia. The devotional attitude of the teller closely resembles that of the Prioress. Her story is marked by simplicity and an undeniable reverence for the subject. Professor Robinson says of it: ". . . the truly reverent spirit of the narrative—which was not dramatically composed for the Nun—should be taken into account by those critics who think of Chaucer as out of sympathy with the religion of his age."[28] The ardent prayer to Mary seems to have come from the heart—and, not unreasonably, Chaucer's, since he is here deeply under the spell of Dante. If the work was written soon after the first trip to Italy when, as Ten Brink believed, "Chaucer was going through an intense religious crisis," we can see the direction his faith was taking at a crucial point. It is this work that persuaded Ten Brink of Chaucer's orthodoxy despite evidences of skepticism: "He was a faithful son of the church, even though he had his own opinions about many things. His rationalistic reflections on religious problems have sometimes a skeptical tinge; but his spiritual needs always led him back again to Christian views, and naturally to the form of Christianity in which he was brought up, viz., the Roman church."[29]

In the *Prioress's Tale* (dated late, about 1390-92), Chaucer retold a "miracle of our Lady." To this work he gave a pathos and religious seriousness untouched by a trace of the satiric note which not even the Prioress herself had escaped in the General Prologue. The poet produced an effective tenderness which he had every intention should move his audience, and he succeeded so well that the most insensitive and coarsest of the travelers were touched—or at any rate so subdued "that wonder was to se."

The same religious tone is notable in the *Parson's Tale*. Its date of composition is undetermined, with scholarly opinion ranging between an early period before 1380 (Skeat) and the poet's later years (Koch). If Chaucer intended that it should serve as the climax of his collection, we can see his state of mind when he reached the end of his masterpiece. For the work, combining a sermon on penitence and a treatise on the Seven

Deadly Sins, closely follows the Catholic confession. (It is worth noting that Chaucer was familiar with the preaching of his time: the *Pardoner's Tale* is carefully worked out to conform to the established technique used in sermons.)

It seems improbable that a pronounced skeptic would have been moved to present—or even been capable of capturing—the spirit of such pious works as these. Certainly they are all strongly accented by an orthodox Christian tone. Professor Stewart, in a study based on actual count and analysis of the lines in Chaucer's work, found that "nearly or quite half of it has a distinct religious or moral tendency."[30]

But perhaps even more striking than this indirect expression of faith in Chaucer's sympathetic portrayal of Constance, St. Cecilia, Hugh of Lincoln, and the Parson is his personal declaration of belief. For frequently Chaucer has spoken on the subject, apart from his role as dramatic artist. An early work, the *ABC*, is a translation, and was undertaken perhaps by request; so we cannot accept it as conclusive evidence of the poet's piety. Yet even his translations, conscientious though they might be, were never artificial or wanting in a spirit of spontaneity. In this early piece which was scarcely more than "a poetic exercise," he exceeds his source in religious fervor; and the expression of devotion to the Virgin is notable for its sincerity and genuine religious spirit, which we may well call Chaucer's own.

In *Troilus and Criseyde,* however, there is no question whose voice is raised in the much discussed epilogue.[31] The passage betrays a true religious seriousness and here Chaucer comes as near a personal confession of faith as in any lines he wrote. Some commentators have taken the long passage, the poet's own addition to the work, as a mere adherence to a literary convention, but the sincerity of expression strongly signifies a personal feeling. According to Professor Robinson, "It is a Christian counsel to fix the heart upon the unfailing love of God. The earnestness of the appeal and the elevation of its mood leave no doubt of Chaucer's essentially religious spirit."[32]

Throughout the work Chaucer appeared to be moved by the story of "double sorwes." But when Troilus's soul reached the eighth sphere in its flight to heaven, Chaucer seemed to renounce the whole doctrine of courtly love that he had adapted to the poignant story. The tale ends in disappointment, tragedy, and disillusionment. Whether the epilogue is inappropriate to the artistic whole is beside the point here. What is important is that it shows the poet was clearly sensitive to a spirit of holiness, and in his heart, for all his general acceptance of the world as it was, felt the need to point earnestly toward a better way of life. The admonition to "yonge, fresshe folkes" to turn away from blind lust and worldly vanity to think on God embodies a deeply religious ideal. In conclusion the poet submits the final most Christian answer to the complex riddle of life:

> And loveth hym, the which that right for love
> Upon a crois, oure soules for to beye,
> First starf, and roos, and sit in hevene above;
> For he nyl falsen no wight, dar I seye,
> That wol his herte al holly on hym leye.
>
> (*TC*, v, 1842-46)

It is what Looten calls the "testament d'écrivain chrétien."[33]

The Christian spirit is likewise present in the short poem called *Truth,* or *Balade de Bon Conseyl,* written, according to a doubtful tradition, on the poet's deathbed.[34] Whether it was the poet's dying counsel is immaterial, for whatever the occasion of its composition, it remains a statement of Christian faith. The renunciation of the world, and its hate and greed, the counsel to seek spiritual truth, the assurance that "trouthe thee shal delivere"—these exhortations are so strictly orthodox that they could have been spoken by an ascetic, but they are Chaucer's, and who can doubt the genuine Catholic spirit behind them? On the basis of this short work alone Professor Root felt justified in describing Chaucer as essentially devout. "That is the Catholic spirit; that is the spirit that actuated Chaucer's life."[35]

It is that spirit, too, which is marked in the penitent declaration, perhaps dictated as death approached, known as the *Retractions*. However conventional was the practice of writing retractions,[36] coming at the close of the *Canterbury Tales* this revocation of all his works except "the translacion of Boece de Consolacione, and othere bookes of legendes of seintes, and omelies, and moralitee, and devocioun" has the tone of sincere Christian repentance. If this prose piece is authentic, Professor Tatlock was right in describing Chaucer as a man who would have been disturbed had he missed absolution, unction, and the viaticum.

There is good reason to believe the *Retractions* is Chaucer's. Thomas Gascoigne, a clergyman who died at Oxford in 1458, left a sheaf of manuscript notes which, in accordance with wishes expressed in his will, were copied into a book called *Liber Veritatum*. In one of these pieces Gascoigne spoke of the practice of deathbed confessions. He warned men not to wait to repent their sins at the end of life when it was too late for redemption. For illustration, he described the last moments of Judas and—may he be forgiven the blasphemy of putting our poet in such unworthy company—Geoffrey Chaucer!

Gascoigne lived at Oxford not far from the Chaucer estates only a generation after the poet's death.[37] Gascoigne claimed to have picked up a current story there from an old manuscript, that has since disappeared, in which the poet was said to have dictated his last work between painful gasps on his deathbed.

Thus many say they repent afterwards, when they cannot wipe away their sins and the evils committed by them; just as Chaucer before his death repeatedly cried out: "Woe is me! woe is me! because I cannot now retract or wipe out those things I wickedly wrote on evil and shameful love of men for women, and now they will be carried on from man to man whether I wish it or not." And thus, lamenting, he died.[38]

Whether a literary convention or not, such a confession would have been natural enough in a medieval man of mature years at the point of death.

Moreover, we should remember that the year was 1400 and

that the turn of the century was regarded by many as the Day of Judgment.

. . . they had almost all a vivid fear of Judgment Day. . . .

As has already been seen, the late Fourteenth Century was a period of disorder and political unrest. But this was as nothing compared to the crisis that was passing in the life of the Church. . . . Monks and visionaries prophesied the end of the world. . . . These forecasts which were much more common than one would at first suspect created a wave of emotionalism that swept over Europe.[39]

Small wonder if thoughtful people looked anxiously to the future, regretting the follies of the past. Small wonder if Chaucer too in old age had become more thoughtful about religion, more concerned with the future life. We may well accept the *Retractions* as the repentance of a man who had shown a keen sense of spiritual values, a man who himself stated simply and clearly that he had set out on a pilgrimage to the shrine at Canterbury with *ful devout corage*.

However, though Chaucer's works give evidence of sincere Christian orthodoxy, there remain a number of skeptical statements to be accounted for. One of two assumptions may be made: either he had periods or moods of unorthodoxy, or he felt at least some force in current questionings.

Assuming the former thesis, Thomas R. Lounsbury[40] took the stand that only in Chaucer's youth can we find an acceptance of the established faith, for in later life, according to this critic, the poet made an emphatic declaration of unbelief[41] that placed him in the position of an outright agnostic. "At the outset he is possibly an unthinking, but to all appearances an unquestioning, believer in the faith in which he has been reared."[42] But the later work Lounsbury finds not only skeptical but hostile to the Church. "It is, moreover, hostile to it in a way that implies an utter disbelief in certain of its tenets, and even a disposition to regard them as full of menace to the future of civilization."[43]

In describing Chaucer as an agnostic in his later life, Lounsbury appears to have based his estimate of the poet on some misconceptions. Kittredge, in his review of Lounsbury's *Studies*

[101]

in Chaucer, saw fallacies in logic and some extreme generalizations which led the critic to misconstrue certain lines taken out of their context.[44] Canon Looten, later, observed similar errors of interpretation.[45] But there remains much to be said about Lounsbury's arguments.

Lounsbury first exposes Chaucer's skeptical attitude toward Scripture. "The critical spirit, for instance, is applied by him to the facts of the Bible as coolly as by the most cold-blooded rationalists or the most scoffing of infidels."[46] Looten rightly points out that Lounsbury rests his argument upon a misinterpretation, for he brings as his only evidence Proserpina's denunciation of Solomon as a "lecchour and an ydolastre." But it is not Chaucer who speaks; it is a heathen. It may be beside the point to ask whether Solomon, not notably pious, deserved to be treated with profound respect; but there is surely no obligation to equate the speech of a character of fiction with the author's personal opinion. Lounsbury admits that the passage rests upon the authority of Scripture itself, but he believes "It would never have been so bluntly stated by a spiritually minded man"![47] As a matter of fact, in the prologue to *Melibee* Chaucer went out of his way to defend the Scripture, protesting against the charges of inconsistency which critics of the Gospels might find in different and sometimes contradictory versions of the Passion. In any case, to make Chaucer a skeptic because his characters may not be orthodox is to forget that he is a dramatic artist.

Lounsbury presents as his best evidence of Chaucer's skepticism the opening lines of the *Legend of Good Women.*

> A thousand tymes have I herd men telle
> That ther ys joy in hevene and peyne in helle,
> And I acorde wel that it ys so;
> But, natheles, yet wot I wel also
> That ther nis noon dwellyng in this contree,
> That eyther hath in hevene or helle ybe,
> Ne may of hit noon other weyes witen,
> But as he hath herd seyd, or founde it writen;
> For by assay ther may no man it preve.

But God forbede but men shulde leve
Wel more thing then men han seen with ye!
Men shal not wenen every thing a lye
But yf himself yt seeth, or elles dooth;
For, God wot, thing is never the lasse sooth,
Thogh every wight ne may it nat ysee.
Bernard the monk ne saugh nat all, pardee!

(*LGW*, 1-16)

I readily agree that here the poet raises a question about the authority of revealed truth, as I shall point out later. But he does not, even by implication, reject such truth. It is a misconception of the passage to affirm that though the author does not deny what is said about heaven and hell, "It is equally noticeable that he does not affirm his belief in it."[48] It seems enough, without further protestations on Chaucer's part, for him to "acorde wel that it ys so."

Furthermore, these lines, compared with contemporary ecclesiastical writing, show that the poet's thinking on immortality in at least one respect was not exceptional, and even in close accord with that of an orthodox preacher of his time. John Bromyard (*fl.* 1390), a Dominican friar educated at Oxford, was one of the great English preachers of the Middle Ages and a contemporary of Chaucer's. In his *Summa Predicantium,* Bromyard composed a theological dictionary intended as a textbook for the clergy. His argument for belief in immortality based on simple faith and rational necessity is significant to a discussion of Chaucer because it is precisely that which Chaucer presents in the Prologue to the *Legend.*

Therefore, let those who have chosen to err in regard to the faith in the manner of the aforementioned unbelievers understand the writings in reliance on which it is necessary to believe things that are not seen. And this is a necessity which proceeds as well from divine justice as from human custom. [He first argues that if there is no after life of rewards and punishments, then God cannot be just.]

Secondly, [we are driven] to this same necessity [to believe in God and the after life] from the daily experience of men, in which we see that a blind man in regard to the way and the sun and the moon and other things which he does not see believes his guide who does see; [we believe] also our father or mother or, if they are dead, others who tell us who our father or mother was—we believe the one who tells us; also about ancient kings or in the case of those reading [to us] chronicles or romances or exploits of Charles and Roland and such, we believe things which after all we have never seen. Therefore, *a fortiori* we ought to believe our guide Christ, who sees clearly, and the Holy Scriptures and those who read and preach about God and the salvation of our souls. Therefore, he who does not believe about the way to heaven and the joys of the good and the punishments of the wicked is more stupid than any blindman who believes a boy. And he who does not believe the things that are read in the Scriptures because he has not seen them is more stupid than any idle listener to the aforesaid exploits.[49]

In short, Bromyard argues the necessity of believing in the unseen on the basis of divine revelation. This is exactly what Chaucer is saying when he insists that men "shal nat wenen every thing a lye But yf himself yt seeth."

The loss of faith noted in the *Legend of Good Women,* Lounsbury assures us, makes it evident that the poet, who professed orthodox faith in his youth, progressed toward a pronounced skepticism in a disillusioned and embittered old age. In the earlier works, including the *Troilus,* the poet is supposed to have been in the religious phase. Lounsbury cites *Troilus* as illustrating Chaucer's acceptance of the established faith and the orthodoxy of his doctrinal opinions: "in this earlier work the direct assertion of belief is stated strongly, though there is no apparent reason for stating it at all. . . . When we come to his later work, there is a far different tone manifested."[50] In the *Knight's Tale,* for example, the critic would have it that Chaucer rejected Boccaccio's description of the flight of the soul because of his loss of religious conviction, therefore interpolating a flippant passage.

But Lounsbury fails to consider the possibility that *Troilus* came later than the *Knight's Tale,* as suggested by Professor

Robinson, who has accepted 1385 as an altogether probable date for the completion of the *Troilus,* and 1382 a less certain but possible date for the *Knight's Tale.* This would reverse the situation and make it necessary to find another reason for Chaucer's rejecting the ascent of Arcite's soul than that the poet had grown away from the theological implications. Professor Robinson believes the omission of the scene easy to understand simply as having been considered unsuitable to the spirit of the one and suitable to the other.[51] Tatlock, too, suggests that Chaucer rejected the passage on the basis of suitability, since "Neither the pagan nor the Christian other-world would have fitted the tone of the *Knight's Tale.*"[52] Similarly, Professor Walter Clyde Curry feels that since nowhere in the *Knight's Tale* Chaucer is concerned with the moral or religious aspects of the situation, "it would be artistically incongruous to postulate any definite resting-place for the released spirit of Arcite."[53] Skeat notes (significantly, if *Troilus* was written first) that the "real reason why Chaucer could not here describe the passage of Arcite's soul to heaven is because he had already copied Boccaccio's description, and had used it with respect to the death of Troilus."[54]

The lines in question from the *Knight's Tale* describe Arcite's death:

> His spirit chaunged hous and wente ther,
> As I cam nevere, I kan nat tellen wher.
> Therfore I stynte, I nam no divinistre;
> Of soules fynde I nat in this registre,
> Ne me ne list thilke opinions to telle
> Of hem, though that they writen wher they dwelle.
>
> (*KnT*, 2809-14)

"Can modern agnosticism," asks Lounsbury, "point to a denial more emphatic . . . of the belief that there exists for us any assurance of the life that is lived beyond the grave?"[55]

It is true that the poet rejects the responsibility of assigning the pagan soul to its final resting place. He excuses himself, claiming ignorance of a place where he happens not to have been. But he does not challenge the doctrine of immortality, as

Lounsbury believed. In fact, the lines lend themselves to an interpretation quite different from Lounsbury's and one which, so far as I know, has not been discussed. Tatlock did suggest the possibility that Chaucer might have been "doubtful as to the eternal destiny of such a virtuous pagan as Arcite,"[56] but no one in connection with this passage has gone fully into the problem of the righteous heathen as it was considered in the Middle Ages, which Chaucer could have had in mind.

We have already seen how many of Chaucer's contemporaries had dealt with the problem,[57] how they had renounced the stern dicta of theologians who condemned the souls of those good people born in pre-Christian times. Arcite was one of these, and who was Chaucer to settle the matter upon which even orthodox churchmen were unable to agree? It is possible that when the poet expressed ignorance of the final resting place of Arcite's soul he was thinking of this question with which medieval people seemed familiar, and writing about it in terms they would clearly understand. The conjecture is at least as plausible as Lounsbury's conviction that the doubt and denial which seemed to him implicit in the passage denote the chief characteristic of Chaucer's mind in the latest and most mature phase of his development.

Besides pointing to Chaucer's outright skeptical expressions as evidence of agnosticism, Lounsbury describes his indifference to the Church as manifest because he looked upon corrupt conditions about him from the comparatively passionless position of a man of letters, whose temper nothing could arouse.[58] The critic has overlooked forthright qualities in a man who was regarded by the centuries immediately succeeding him—the fifteenth, sixteenth, and occasionally the seventeenth—as a *moralist* and *reformer*.[59] He has also ignored the depth of Chaucer's satire, when he can characterize him as looking placidly upon the iniquity notoriously prevalent in the fourteenth century. "So far is he from denouncing it, that he brings before us his villains of every station without a word of reprobation. . . . But nowhere does he, when speaking in his own person, exhibit the slightest emotion of any sort. For his

[106]

religious rascals he seems, in fact, to have had a sort of liking; at any rate, he has invariably something to say in their favor."[60]

To be sure, Chaucer may compliment the Prioress on her table manners, the Monk on his skill in hunting, the Friar on his success in extracting farthings from poor widows, but only the most naive will regard these observations as evidence of liking on his part. Each compliment is tinctured with venom. And what of the poet's description of the Pardoner? What had he to say in favor of the man whom he pictured as physically repulsive, whom he exposed as a charlatan and hypocrite? Here there is no trace of the kindly nature of a poet who has been described as benevolent and cheerful[61] and characterized by gaiety, harmless fun, and a contented faith;[62] it certainly does not bear out Lounsbury's insistence that Chaucer's "contempt is invariably good-humored."[63]

Inconsistently enough, Lounsbury later charges Chaucer with hostility to the Church for giving increasing prominence to the immorality and fraudulence of those men purporting to protect and teach the faith.

One characteristic which not unusually accompanies the decline of faith in the individual is in him very conspicuous. This is the prominence given to the falsity and fraud of those who have professedly devoted themselves to the advancement of the cause of Christianity. The moral degradation of the men who have entered the service of the church for the purpose of serving their own interests are the things which largely attract his attention. . . . [He] found later his keenest delight in the exposure of that dry rot in religion when men no longer practise what they preach, or even understand what they profess to believe.[64]

Chaucer's indictments of the clergy, bitter as they are, argue rather for devotion to his faith than antagonism toward it. His indignation over the unworthy rascals who violated their sacred oaths bespeaks a sincere respect for an ideal that he would not willingly see abused. But none of his denunciations involves criticism of Church or dogma or, indeed, any worthy representatives of his faith. "C'est au contraire parce qu'il a de l'état réligieux une haute et juste conception qu'il fustige ceux qui malgré leur voeu solennel cessent d'y conformer leurs moeurs," says Looten in his defense.[65] He was as kindly toward the Prioress as he was ironical with the Monk, as reverent in his attitude toward the Second Nun as scornful toward the Friar. He spared neither Franciscan nor Benedictine, but it should not be forgotten that the model character in the *Canterbury Tales* is a parson. Anticlericalism was common enough among orthodox Catholics throughout a century that was notorious for corruption of the clergy. There is no dearth of material, recorded by churchmen themselves, to testify to the shocking conditions existing in the fourteenth-century Church, as Coulton has shown at length.[66] But anticlericalism is not skepticism, and Chaucer on this basis no more deserves the accusation of infidelity than Gower and Deschamps, who harped on the decay of the clergy far more insistently.

True, Lounsbury admits that conventional attacks on the clergy were commonplace, but he charges Chaucer with something more subtle and malicious than criticism of corruption in the Orders. He sees special significance in the heterodox views that the poet puts in the mouths of his most disreputable characters.[67] But these are counterbalanced by a proportionate number of professions of faith on the part of the devout members of the company and—more importantly—in his own person.

From all evidence Chaucer appears to have been a good Catholic, with a sincere feeling for spiritual values. Why, then, has he been accused of skepticism even by scholars who are in general accord as to his essentially Christian spirit?[68]

Admittedly, in Chaucer's works are certain lines that lend themselves to a variety of interpretations concerning his religious belief. Some of these lines are undeniably skeptical: we find him challenging God's foresight (Philomela, *LGW*, 2228-37), raising questions about the soul (*KnT*, 2809-14), and discussing the existence of heaven and hell (Pro, *LGW*, 1-16) —controversial subjects, unexpectedly introduced in works of a professed Christian of the Middle Ages.

[108]

In what ways can these contradictions be explained?

Undoubtedly Chaucer was a man whose nature, mind, and experience, we have seen, predisposed him to a broad outlook. Let us glance at his liberal view of notions held by many people of his day: He distrusted judicial astrology, a science then generally approved; he violently satirized alchemists, regarded with respect by intelligent men of his time; and he poked fun at fairy-lore and magic, which a considerable number of his contemporaries accepted.

Chaucer's criticism of astrology is noteworthy, for the heavenly bodies played so integral a part in medieval daily life that the science of the stars was highly regarded. Florence M. Grimm has shown what a reputable position astrologers held in the Middle Ages. "Astrology, as a science and a system of divination, exerted a profound influence over the mediaeval mind. No court was without its practicing astrologer and the universities all had their professors of astrology."[69]

In very early times astrology had been looked upon as black magic, and it was not until the science of Aristotle and the Arabians was introduced in the twelfth century that it was approved as a respectable field of knowledge.[70] Thomas Aquinas, while rejecting planetary influence over the will, admitted its effect on the body and subsequently on the emotions.[71] Since celestial bodies affect men physically, he said, their emotions become involved; while human will can supersede planetary control, most men are guided by emotion and consequently "astrologers are able to foretell the truth in the majority of cases, especially in a general way."[72]

T. O. Wedel has traced the growing interest in astrology through the Middle Ages, showing that by the fourteenth century the more learned a man was in astronomy and astrology the greater was his enthusiasm for the pseudo-science.[73] And we find a number of Chaucer's contemporaries asserting belief in it.

A man of such intelligence as the God-fearing Gower accepted some of the marvels of astrology. He pronounced God's power as being above that of the stars, but he could not reject their influence on daily life. Gower saw in the "Mones disposicion" the cause of the restless nature of Englishmen, the reason "thei travaile in every lond." Astrology, he said,

in juggementz acompteth
Theffect, what every sterre amonteth.

(*CA*, vii, 81-82)

Deschamps repeatedly condemned astrological "magic" but his abhorrence seems to have been based solely on religious grounds; intellectually he accepted astrology and even a moderate application of judicial astrology in determining harvests, the favorable time to take medicine, and the outcome of other human affairs which he believed to be dependent on the influence of the stars.[74]

Langland takes all manner of people to task for shirking their work, from the tillers of the soil who no longer produce harvests to astronomers—astrologers, that is, in the modern sense—who do not apply their art:

Astronomyens al daye in here art faillen,
That whilom warned men by-fore what shoulde by-falle after.

(*PP*, C, xviii, 96-97)

And again, describing the different levels of society, he explains that it is the lot of some to labor, some to till,

And somme to dyuyne and dyuyde numbres to kenne,
And craftely to compassen and colours to make.
And somme to seo and to seye what sholde by-falle
Bothe of wele and of wo and be war by-fore,
As astronomyens thorw astronomye.

(*PP*, C, xxii, 240-44)

On the whole, most people of Chaucer's day believed in astrology, especially in its importance to physical well-being. According to the medieval theory of physiology and the four humors or "complexions," planetary influences were so important that a doctor was often deemed not quite competent unless he had an accurate knowledge of the stars. John of Burgundy made the complaint of certain doctors that they were

[110]

"allefully ignorant in the sience of Astronomy, the which science is in phisik wonder nedefull."[75] Chaucer's Doctor of Physic was as a matter of course "grounded in astronomye." From Galen on down, the proportion of humors (blood, yellow bile, black bile, and phlegm—corresponding to the four elements: air, fire, earth, and water) was assumed to be influenced by the position of the planets.[76] So deeply implanted was this belief that in medieval records we find few doctors who are not designated also as "astronomers." In the unique work[77] of Simon de Phares,[78] a fifteenth-century astrologer who in defense of his science compiled a record of more than a thousand astrologers, the writer lists almost every astrologer as a practicing physician. Of Galen he says:

Sovereign doctor and astrologer, he well pointed out at that time in his works that no one is worthy of being called doctor unless he be well instructed in the science of the stars. . . . Among other wise things, he said in the book *Les Jours cretiques*: "Let every doctor know that when the Moon unites with the fortunate stars, maladies are brought to a good end, and by its conjunction with contrary stars opposite and evil effects are caused, and therefore the good doctor must first of all consider at what point the Moon is, to determine whether it is a new, or full Moon, for then the humors and marrows increase."[79]

Simon mentions at least fifteen astrologers who were consulted by Chaucer's king, Richard II. In 1390-91 the English ruler engaged one of them to compile a work on astrology, entitled *Liber regis Ricardi secundi,* a technical study of horoscopy.[80] He even entrusted astrologers with official matters, as in the case of Philippe de Bardiz (known as Brandis de Navarre), whom he sent for to advise the expedition to Ireland in 1399. How heavily Richard relied on astrology in affairs of state is verified by Kervyn de Lettenhove, who believes the young ruler's confidence in prophecies attaching to his birth (on Twelfth Night) gave him a recklessness and arrogance that led, at least in part, to his downfall.[81]

Chaucer too may have believed in astrology in a general way like most of his contemporaries, as Wedel and Tatlock have insisted,[82] but at least twice he made it clear that he was skeptical of certain applications of it. While his characters sometimes assume a nature deriving from planetary influence, and though astrology figures in his conjectures about Fortune, free will, and predestination, his most extensive astrological references seem to be for dramatic and artistic effect.

The poet did not pass judgment on subjects lightly. He had enough interest in astronomy to write a scientific treatise on it, which has been called "the earliest extant work in English upon an elaborate scientific instrument."[83] He called himself a "lewd compilator of the labour of olde astrologiens," and whether he actually had in his hand the work of Messahala, eighth-century Arabian astronomer, or whether he used Vincent of Beauvais and other secondary sources, his *Treatise on the Astrolabe* is a painstaking if simplified study and conforms to medieval knowledge of astronomy and astrology. In Part II he devoted a section to current beliefs regarding the horoscope, describing how a planet in its ascendancy was said to "be shapen for to be fortunat or infortunat." But the author was skeptical of this sort of thing: "Natheles these ben observaunces of judicial matere and rytes of payens, in whiche my spirit hath no feith, ne knowing of her *horoscopum*." (II, 4)

In the *Franklin's Tale* he had already treated the subject less scientifically but with a scorn that the scholars have not altogether succeeded in explaining away.[84] Rites of astrology were in Chaucer's opinion "swiche illusiouns and swiche meschaunces As hethen folk useden in thilke dayes." A book of "magyk natureel" he scorned:

> Which book spak muchel of the operaciouns
> Touchynge the eighte and twenty mansiouns
> That longen to the moone, and swich folye
> As in oure dayes is nat worth a flye.
>
> (*FraT*, 1129-32)

It is particularly interesting that Chaucer introduced his critical opinion here, when "magyk natureel" was an artistic necessity. The power of astrological magic was taken in all seriousness by many medieval people, and forecasting of the future by the stars and their relative positions in the heavens was widely accepted. In his suggestion that natural magic was worthless "folye," Chaucer was somewhat more critical than most men of his time. Tatlock, who believes Chaucer's opinion of astrology was no more advanced than that of many of his contemporaries, states however in conclusion: "He was greatly interested and in general believed there was a good deal in it, though his view probably varied from time to time; as to some of its applications in his own day he was sceptical and strongly disapproving."[85] Certainly, even if he accepted some kind of astrological fatalism, he frankly doubted a very satisfactory forecasting of events by the stars, for

> mennes wittes ben so dulle
> That no wight kan wel rede it atte fulle.
>
> (MLT, 202-3)

He may not have been unique in his occasional opposition to astrology on philosophical grounds—like Gower, Barbour, Bradwardine, Rolle, Trevisa, Langland, or on the basis of religious abhorrence—like Wyclif, Petrarch, Groote, Deschamps; nevertheless, he adopts an attitude not of general acquiescence of his time but, rather, enlightened opinion of the few.

Alchemy is another "science" practiced by medieval men about which Chaucer's contemporaries wrote and talked. "That the profession was not at this time a disreputable one and that the Government was inclined to look on it with a kindly eye is indicated by the curious case of Thomas of York (1337), who asked for, and was apparently given, an opportunity to demonstrate 'la science de Alconemie.' "[86] A number of the writers of the time referred to alchemy as a science. Gower, for example, described its processes without any indication that he discountenanced it:

> And also with gret diligence
> Thei fonden thilke experience,
> Which cleped is Alconomie,
> Wherof the Silver multeplie

Thei made and ek the gold also.
And forto telle how it is so,
Of bodies sevene in special
With foure spiritz joynt withal
Stant the substance of this matiere.

(*CA*, IV, 2457-65)

Langland, while disapproving of alchemy as a science designed to trick good people, testifies that it was commonly practiced, warning against

Experimentz of alkenamye   the poeple to deceyue,
If thow thinke to Dowel   dele ther-with neuere.

(*PP*, B, x, 212-13)

In the *Canon's Yeoman's Tale*, believed to have been written late in his life, Chaucer described the alchemical processes with such careful detail that there can be no doubt he had given considerable thought to the subject, even if, using Vincent of Beauvais as his chief source,[87] he had not read as widely as has been supposed. Certainly he had made up his own mind what he thought of it as a legitimate science. Through the Yeoman he gives a lively account of the disreputable dealings of one dishonest master of the science. As the innocent victim of the anecdote, the Yeoman can vent strong feelings against the swindler by whom he had been humiliatingly duped.

It has been suggested that Chaucer himself had been swindled by such a trick.[88] But whatever relation the story may bear to personal experience, there is no question of Chaucer's expression of aversion to the pseudo-science. The *Canon's Yeoman's Tale* is among his most skilful stories, the Yeoman one of his most convincing characters; there could hardly be a more effective criticism of a practice that the writer looked upon with distaste. From the dramatic appearance of the Yeoman, when he galloped wildly up to join the Canterbury company, to the final warning that "no man bisye hym this art for to seche," the tale is a sharp attack on all followers of the "slidynge science." Though alchemy was already in some disrepute, especially with such churchmen as Langland, a large number of people still believed in it, and Chaucer's exposé of at least one fraudulent

[114]

practitioner of the "false craft" indicates independent judgment of a man who was far from gullible.

Astrology and alchemy were sciences accepted in general by the average Englishmen of the fourteenth century. But the fairy kingdom is another story; when we come to fairy-lore, we have something they not only accepted but took to their hearts. Addison has said in a famous *Spectator* essay (July 1, 1712) it was the "naturally fanciful" temper of the English which disposed them more than other peoples to "many wild notions and visions," so that in the time of his forefathers "There was not a village in England that had not a ghost in it, the church-yards were all haunted; every large common had a circle of fairies belonging to it; and there was scarce a shepherd to be met with who had not seen a spirit." Certainly neighborhood gossip abounded with mysterious elves, witches, and trolls.

A favorite theme was the union of human beings with supernatural spirits. The most extensive and elaborate treatment of such a union, *Melusine,* by Jean d'Arras, appeared in Chaucer's own time. Jean, under the patronage of the royal house of France in the time of Charles VI, compiled the materials of the story for the Duchess of Bar (Mary, daughter of the French King John), who asked her brother, Duke of Berry and Auvergne, to command Jean to write it down. Accordingly he set to work November 23, 1389.[89]

Jean treated the matter factually, emphasizing the dependability of his sources and urging his readers to accept the story. In his preface he asserts:

. . . he is not wyse that . . . weneth that the meruaylles that ben thrugh the vniuersal world, may nat be true, as it is said of the thinges that men call ffayrees/and as it is of many other thinges whereof we may not haue the knowleche of alle them. . . . I putte them fourth into this termes byfore you/to thende that the grette meruaylles that ben conteyned in this present hystory may be byleue.[90]

At the end of the long tale, Jean reiterates its authenticity:

. . . I haue putte my self to myn vtermost power to rede & loke ouer the Cronykles & many bokes of auncyent hystoryes, to thende that I might knowe the trouth of the forsaid matere.

[115]

Therfore yf I haue wryton or shewed ony thing that to som semeth neyther possible to be nor credible, I beseche them to pardonne me. For as I fele & vnderstond by the Auctours of gramaire & phylosophye they repute and hold this present hystorye for a true Cronykle & thinges of the fayry. . . . For there is found in many hystoryes Fayries that haue be maryed & had many children/but how this may be the humayn creature may not conceyue.[91]

Melusine, fairy woman married to Raimund of Lusignan, was said to return to Lusignan whenever the castle was to have a new master or one of her descendants was about to die. There is evidence that this legend was taken seriously by intelligent people. Jean testifies that reliable clerks had claimed to have seen her, as: Evan of Wales (*d.* 1378), whose father died at the hands of Edward III and who himself was hated in England for his claims to the Welsh crown; Creswel, Captain of the English forces who fought at Lusignan; Perceval de Cologne, chamberlain of the King of Cyprus (Pierre of Lusignan), who likewise swore that the king had confided to him he had seen Melusine—and had died three days later, January 17, 1369.

A story attributed to Thomas of Erceldoune (*c.* 1296) and still called by his name was probably written between 1388 ana 1400.[92] Like *Melusine,* the story tells of the union of a mortal man with a supernatural woman, but this time the scene is in "another cuntre," never called fairyland in the story but corresponding to medieval notions of what the land of fairies was like. When, after three years, the fairy queen returns Thomas to his homeland, she makes a number of prophecies, some historical—the Battles of Bannockburn and Durham, and the story of David Bruce; some unhistorical—the battles of the Scots and the English, and the death of Black Agnes of Dunbar. Here, as so often in medieval fairy-lore, historical fact mingles with fiction. These prophecies appeared in manuscript for the next two centuries. That the medieval readers took their author seriously is suggested by Professor Rupert Taylor's discovery of frequent references made by fourteenth-century writers to such predictions as circulated under the name of Thomas of Erceldoune.[93]

[116]

Among people as a whole, the most popular fairy stories were those that treated the legend of Arthur. Englishmen still treasured the memory of King Arthur their one-time ruler, and cherished the legends about him. Modern historians believe there was such a leader in the late fifth or early sixth century; it is natural that many medieval people believed also the legends that persistently clustered around his name in history and story.

People who still talked about Arthur and the supernatural adventures of his knights—Chaucer refers to the book of Lancelot as one that "wommen holde in ful greet reverence"—would be likely to accept magic and all kinds of wonder. Professor Robinson believes that "The association of the Knights of the Round Table with *Fairye* was natural, in view of the many tales of enchantment and other-world adventure in the Arthurian romances. Moreover, in the case of King Arthur there was a definite tradition that after he was wounded in his last battle he was carried away to the land of the fairies, whence he would some day return to rule his people."[94]

One of the most interesting, and often called the best, of medieval English romances concerns one of Arthur's knights, *Sir Gawain and the Green Knight,* written about 1370. The poet was either a noble or connected with a noble's household, a man of genius, refinement, and intelligence. He introduces his story with a historical reference, to Brutus who founded Britain, and he places his story in the time of Arthur, "Of all Britain's kings the noblest." Here was a man of culture and learning, who soberly asserted that

> More marvels
> Befell in those fields since the days of their finding
> Than anywhere else upon earth that I know of,
>
> (*GGK*, 22-24)

and who implied belief in

> an adventure
> Strange and surprising, as some men consider,
> A strange thing among all the marvels of Arthur.
>
> (*GGK*, 26-28)

[117]

There is some indication that other educated people took stock in tales of wonder, magic, or the supernatural. Even the worldly-wise and sometimes skeptical Froissart reflects seriously upon a story told him by the squire of the Earl of Foix. The squire related how his master, who one day had sat alone for a long while, sad and pensive, explained that he was troubled because his men, fighting at Juberothe in Portugal, had come to grief. Ten days later it was learned that this indeed was true, the Earl's country having suffered its most disastrous loss in a hundred years. The squire confided that the Earl always knew at once all that happened in distant parts. Commenting on this extraordinary assertion, Froissart writes: "Than he is a devyner, quod I, or els he hathe messangers that flyeth with the wynde, or he muste nedes have some crafte."[95] The squire then told how his master came by this skill, through a mysterious "spirit" whom he called by name, Orthon. That Froissart was impressed is apparent in his preface:

It is great marveyle to consyder one thynge, the whiche was shewed me in therle of Foix house at Ortayse, of hym that en-fourmed me of the busynesse at Juberothe: he shewed me one thyng that I have oftentymes thought on sithe, and shall do as longe as I lyve.[96]

Gower, too, while averse to necromancy and magic of all kinds, admitted that it was all right when properly used:

> For these craftes, as I finde,
> A man mai do be weie of kinde,
> Be so it be to good entente.
>
> (CA, vi, 1303-5)

Here, Wedel believes, "Gower steps beyond the limits set by orthodox doctrine in condoning the practice of magic when employed for a good purpose."[97]

Langland, on the contrary, stood as always on the side of the Church; he saw no good in magic in any of its forms. But in his condemnation he testified to the ability of the sorcerer to raise up the devil, a feat commonly supposed to be within the power of magic.[98]

[118]

Nigromancye and perimancie   the pouke to rise maketh;
Yif thou thenche Dowel   dele with hem neuere.

(PP, A, xi, 158-59)

It is characteristic of Chaucer's independence that he was
not, like many of his time, taken in by tales of wonder and by
fairy-lore. In the *Tale of Sir Thopas* the poet did not disavow
belief in the fairy queen, but by making her the "lemman" of
the preposterous knight in a burlesque he evidently regarded
her with amusement. In the *Wife of Bath's Tale* he cast some
doubt on the existence of the "elf-queene, with hir joly compaignye"; he declared one could no longer see such a creature
as an elf; he implied that King Arthur himself was only a
legendary figure. Yet, he assures us, Britons still spoke very
honorably of their ancient king:

In th'olde dayes of the Kyng Arthour,
Of which that Britons speken greet honour,
Al was this land fulfild of fayerye.
The elf-queene, with hir joly compaignye,
Daunced ful ofte in many a grene mede.
This was the olde opinion, as I rede;
I speke of manye hundred yeres ago.
But now kan no man se none elves mo.

(WBT, 857-64)

Chaucer seemed to wish to disclaim responsibility for stories
he perhaps doubted but which were widely accepted, as those
dealing with fairies. Notice that he made it clear he did not
vouch for them. It was an *olde opinion* that the queen and her
fairies danced in the mead. If Proserpina and the fairy band
disported in the aged January's garden, it was *as men say* or as
one may in *stories rede*. The story of Chauntecleer, he says slyly,
is as true as the book of Lancelot. And even at the risk of de-
stroying the willing suspension of disbelief important to his
plot, he interrupts the *Franklin's Tale* to emphasize that in his
own opinion magic is a fraud. This disclaiming of any exact
knowledge of fairies and magic is in striking contrast to other
tellers of marvelous tales who went to great pains to establish
authentic sources and to vouch for them.

[119]

Chaucer puts the same critical opinion in the mind of one of his characters, for the Parson is equally scornful of magic. His strong feeling grows out of religious abhorrence, not exceptional in men of the Church, but the Parson's charge against "false enchauntours" for their evil practices is an index of the kinds of magic to which people apparently subscribed.

But lat us go now to thilke horrible sweryng of adjuracioun and conjuracioun, as doon thise false enchauntours or nigromanciens in bacyns ful of water, or in a bright swerd, in a cercle, or in a fir, or in a shulderboon of a sheep./I kan nat seye but that they doon cursedly and dampnably agayns Crist and al the feith of hooly chirche./
What seye we of hem that bileeven on divynailes, as by flight or by noyse of briddes, or of beestes, or by sort, by geomancie, by dremes, by chirkynge of dores, or crakkynge of houses, by gnawynge of rattes, and swich manere wrecchednesse?/

(*ParsT*, 603-5)

These lines cannot be traced to any literary source; there is little doubt that Chaucer was enumerating superstitions he had heard about and perhaps noted among the people he knew.

Chaucer, in his attitude toward these popular beliefs, shows himself somewhat at variance with many of his fellow men. But does the independent judgment of a practical, intelligent man who was not taken in by medieval "marvels" incline him toward agnosticism? Not necessarily, though it helps explain his tendency to weigh the pros and cons, to apply rational standards to philosophical and religious problems, to take the side of advanced learned thought of his generation.

Much of his concern with these problems, and especially his interest in skeptical ideas, may have grown out of the circumstances of Chaucer's life which threw him with the men who were talking about them. He certainly knew Gower, Deschamps —if not personally, at least through his work and a friendly message from across the sea, and perhaps Froissart, Walsingham, and Wyclif. Among his associates were a number of Wyclifites, like Clifford and Stury, who we know were close to him. Scholars are now generally agreed that Chaucer was not a follower of Wyclif, though he subscribed to some ideas that at one time or another have won him the charge of Lollardy.[99] But even this interest in itself is significant, for the Lollards are known to have created an atmosphere that bred criticism of traditional beliefs, as Tatlock was well aware when he spoke of Wyclifism as the "natural background of skepticism for an intellectually independent Englishman of the late fourteenth century."[100]

Equally important in Chaucer's background are his travels. From the time of his first visit to Italy in 1372-73, the Italian influence was so pronounced that the years 1372-84 are often referred to as his "Italian period." Italian scholars were notoriously freethinking,[101] and Chaucer may well have felt the spirit of skepticism which was more prevalent in Italy than elsewhere. Coulton observes: "In Petrarch's time—that is, in the Italy that Chaucer knew—atheism and materialistic philosophies were extremely fashionable; before the Reformation had come, the 'advanced' scholars of the University of Padua seem to have been as unorthodox as those of the present day."[102]

These circumstances of his life contribute to an explanation of Chaucer's awareness of living issues, his readiness to introduce them into his work—often quite gratuitously. If to the poet discretion was the better part of valor—because of superlative tact, common sense, or prudent neutrality[103]—yet he was not always passive or silent and did on occasion speak out upon matters he felt strongly about. His reaction to vital problems of the period is clear enough to indicate what thoughts passed through his mind during those hours he devoted to his books. He seems to have been troubled more than once by philosophical doubts and questionings, for more often than not he was serious in mood; almost always his works are more serious than the sources from which he drew his materials.[104]

In view of certain lines he wrote, it would seem that Chaucer did not always find it possible to square his faith with his reason, especially in regard to some of the dogmas. In the General Prologue his allusion to the "ercedekenes curs" and

[121]

"assoillyng" (lines 654-56, 660-61) is so equivocal that the poet's meaning is susceptible of some doubt. It may be only a criticism of the abuses of the clergy, though the reference to excommunication and absolution, however guarded, implies skepticism of their efficacy. Professor Robinson takes the passage on absolution as an expression of unmistakable doubt,[105] as does Tatlock: "Chaucer seems to speak lightly and skeptically of both excommunication and absolution. Both passages show an attitude of doubt toward the power of the keys as commonly understood in Chaucer's day."[106]

There are other lines in Chaucer, however, which point more clearly to the poet's attitudes. Lounsbury was justified in citing the opening lines of the *Legend of Good Women* as evidence of the poet's rational attitude toward religion. I do not agree that the poet went so far as to reject his faith or to challenge the promise of an after life, for he clearly states that he believes "it ys so." Yet

> wot I wel also
> That ther nis noon dwellyng in this contree,
> That eyther hath in hevene or helle ybe.
>
> (*LGW*, 4-6)

In spite of simple faith in a life after death, Chaucer speculated upon the substance of things hoped for, the evidence of things not seen. In so many words he shows the same rational spirit that Caesarius of Heisterbach charged a young girl of the thirteenth century with revealing when she asked: "Who on returning from that place has shown us what he saw?"[107] The case of this girl, condemned by her priest to lie in unhallowed ground unless she could accept without question the doctrine he taught her, was cited as an example of those whose faith grievously wavered. Chaucer's faith was not grounded any more strongly. "For by assay ther may no man it preve." Though he affirmed his belief, he acknowledged that no one, not even St. Bernard himself had ocular proof. Within a decade of the poet's own life span, a rationalist doggedly argued that there was no visible evidence of revealed truth[108]—and died at the stake for a transgression hardly greater than Chaucer in this passage confesses.

That these lines had been set down carefully and intended to reach an audience, not by chance or fancy but by absorbing interest in the subject, there can be little doubt. The lines are not conspicuously appropriate to the spirit of the love-vision which follows; and the poet made a significant change in the literary source that he was using here, Froissart's *Joli Buisson de jonece.*

Froissart too had heard about impossible things; likewise had he not found anyone who had been an eyewitness to them.

> I have heard talk
> Of the Fountain of Youth,
> Also of invisible stones;
> But these are impossible things,
> For never have I seen that one
> (By the faith I owe St. Marcelli)
> Who has said: "I have actually been there."[109]

Chaucer adopts this theme in the opening lines of the *Legend,* in so striking a parallel to the rhetorical character of the introduction to *Joli Buisson de jonece* that he was almost certainly imitating Froissart. But he departs radically from his source to bring into a collection of love stories the question of immortality, speculating not upon the fountain of youth but upon life after death. Why did he substitute a serious theological discussion for the French poet's lyric on youth, which would have been more in keeping with the stories of love and lovers? The only answer appears to be the poet's interest in a basic matter of faith.

In his subsequent discussion, after clearly stating his belief in the promised joy in heaven and pain in hell, he says bluntly that no one had, after all, been either in heaven or hell and come back to tell us about it. No one, he says, knows anything at all about it—and here he rejects by implication a large body of vision literature taken by churchmen and all good Catholics as evidence not perhaps of actual existence in heaven but at least of an authentic glimpse into the beyond. These lines, even

[123]

if they do not betoken any disloyalty to the Church in which their author had been reared, reveal a questioning spirit and free intelligence characteristic of a thoughtful, independent mind.

A problem more disturbing to Chaucer than immortality was that of God's justice, which raised further questions in his inquiring mind about the tangled mysteries of life. To reconcile the existence of evil with a divine plan and to justify the ways of God to man had perplexed philosophers from time immemorial. While translating the *Consolation of Philosophy,* Chaucer found Boethius grappling with the enigma: "If the order of things is ordained by God, then is He responsible for evil as well as good?" (V, Pr. 3) The writer poses the question, arguing that such a proposition leaves man no hope, no reason to pray (a conclusion commonly reached by those who had struggled with the idea of determinism),[110] but Lady Philosophy answers to his satisfaction. In Chaucer's work we find an echo of the question, but not the answer. In *Troilus and Criseyde*—note that the poet, in the long discussion of predestination, foreknowledge, and free will, again departs from his source to interpolate a serious question where it is not at all called for by his original—the problem is left unresolved. Troilus, considering the good and evil in the world and man's helplessness to avert fate, blames the vagaries of fortune. The fatalism may or may not be Chaucer's. Professor Robinson urges caution in estimating the import of the passage: "It is not to be inferred that Chaucer himself was a fatalist." But he adds significantly: "At the same time it is to be observed that more than once in the *Troilus* the reader is made to feel a deep sense of overruling Destiny."[111]

To be sure, fatalism is not skepticism; nor did the Church make belief in free will *or* predestination an obligation. But medieval churchmen did try to unify the spiritual and material, attempting to reconcile conflicting attitudes, and the teachings of the Church sought to find compatibility between human freedom and divine providence—something it was given to man to understand only on faith.[112] Confusion, fatalism, questioning

[124]

of providence, and even loss of faith—especially in the efficacy of prayer[113]—could result from inability to resolve the problem of determinism. St. Augustine had argued that contemplation of human misery and death and the Christian teaching makes one indifferent.[114] Such indifference often marked the attitude of the man disturbed by the problem of free will and predestination, because there was inherent in determinism an eternal conflict.[115]

It was such a conflict that troubled Troilus. Of course the opinions of the brooding Troilus are not necessarily Chaucer's. Troilus, beset as he is by misfortune, is understandably resentful. What man, desolated by disappointment and upset by conflicting emotions, has not been moved to indulge in hotheaded assertions he did not in cooler moments believe? It would be unfair to seek reasoned judgment in Troilus's words; least of all would it be fair to attribute them to the poet. But the exposition of good and evil and God's foresight in the *Troilus,* a section added after the earlier manuscript of the work was completed, attests Chaucer's interest. His conclusion elsewhere seems to lie in the general optimism of his own nature and his trust in an ultimate good as the final goal of ill, the "trouthe" that "shal delivere." Nevertheless, he is well aware of a theological problem here; from Troilus's point of view, if there is evil, it is evil which God has predestined and for which Troilus, having "no fre chois," is not therefore personally responsible.

> Syn God seeth every thyng, out of doutaunce,
> And hem disponyth, thorugh his ordinaunce,
> In hire merites sothly for to be,
> As they shul comen by predestyne.
>
> (*TC,* IV, 963-66)

Lacking any sense of personal guilt, Troilus feels neither repentance nor submission to divine will. He does not accept on faith the churchmen's assurance that in the final analysis God's inscrutable purpose will be made clear. So far as he is able to see, Fortune is wilful and her favors distributed unjustly. Professor Stewart finds here a note of complete pessimism.

Only the ending keeps *Troilus and Criseyde* from being one of the most pessimistic productions of English literature, and this only by what seems to modern minds begging the question. Boldly abandoning this earth to injustice and wrong, Chaucer puts his trust for Troilus and for all mankind in a heaven from which our petty turmoils here seem only a subject for laughter. . . . This, I might remark, is a good optimistic solution for the universe as a whole. But it is a hard judgment on our poor little earth to be left the prey of the false fickleness of the world, and it is obviously small comfort to anyone who has no immediate confidence in a future state.[116]

The issue of justice was further confused for Chaucer by the apparently arbitrary reward of good and evil, without any fair plan of retribution. It was—and is—a common complaint of man, and we find it in Chaucer's *Boece*:

"What unreste may ben a worse confusioun than that gode men han somtyme adversite and somtyme prosperite, and schrewes also han now thingis that they desiren and now thinges that thei haten?"

(*Bo*, IV, Pr. 6, 196-201)

Chaucer brings up the problem in the *Knight's Tale*, a free adaptation of Boccaccio's *Teseide*, into which he interpolates many philosophical reflections not even hinted at in his source. Note especially Palamon's long soliloquy, when, imprisoned and shut off from the "fresshe Emelye" whom he loves, he hotly protests his fate. Inconsolable, with more bitterness than faith he calls on divine justice:

> "O crueel goddes that governe
> This world with byndyng of youre word eterne,
> And writen in the table of atthamaunt
> Youre parlement and youre eterne graunt,
> What is mankynde moore unto you holde
> Than is the sheep that rouketh in the folde?
> For slayn is man right as another beest,
> And dwelleth eek in prison and arreest,
> And hath siknesse and greet adversitee,
> And ofte tymes giltelees, pardee."

(*KnT*, 1303-12)

Palamon, as perhaps also Chaucer (who does not at any rate reprove his hero for lack of pious submission as other medieval writers were prone to do) despaired over the wilful punishment of guiltless men, of whose fate he could see no ultimate source. He failed to understand by what justice the divine will seemed to bestow order upon all things in the universe except only man. It is again the voice of Boethius:

> "O thow makere of the wheel that bereth the sterres, which that art festnyd to thi perdurable chayer, and turnest the hevene with a ravysschynge sweigh, and constreynest the sterres to suffren thi lawe. . . . O thou governour, governynge alle thynges by certein ende, whi refusestow oonly to governe the werkes of men by duwe manere?"
>
> (*Bo*, i, Me, 5, 1-5, 34-37)

For all their faith and hope and intellect that raise them above the level of the animal world, men are no safer from cruel destruction than are beasts whose fate seems far less painful than men's. Innocence and goodness count for little:

> "What governance is in this prescience,
> That giltelees tormenteth innocence?
> And yet encresseth this al my penaunce,
> That man is bounden to his observaunce,
> For Goddes sake, to letten of his wille,
> Ther as a beest may al his lust fulfille.
> And whan a beest is deed he hath no peyne;
> But man after his deeth moot wepe and pleyne,
> Though in this world he have care and wo.
> Withouten doute it may stonden so.
> The answere of this lete I to dyvynys,
> But wel I woot that in this world greet pyne ys.
> Allas, I se a serpent or a theef,
> That many a trewe man hath doon mescheef,
> Goon at his large, and where hym list may turne."
>
> (*KnT*, 1313-27)

To the unhappy Palamon it seemed too much to bear that man must not only suffer in this world but in the next. His observation that too often the innocent suffer at the hands of the wicked, and the wicked go free, was not original, for he was wrestling with a universal, an eternal problem—one of which Chaucer was well aware and which, more than once, gave him pause. Palamon could give the riddle of life over to the theologians, but he could not believe in a just providence.

In the opening lines of *Philomela* in the *Legend of Good Women* is another striking challenge to God's foresight. Here too Chaucer raises a problem, of which there are no hints in corresponding passages of his Latin and French originals.

> Thow yevere of the formes, that hast wrought
> This fayre world, and bar it in thy thought
> Eternaly, er thow thy werk began,
> Why madest thow, unto the slaunder of man,
> Or, al be that it was nat thy doing,
> As for that fyn, to make swich a thyng,
> Whi sufferest thow that Tereus was bore,
> That is in love so fals and so forswore,
> That, fro this world up to the firste hevene
> Corrumpeth, whan that folk his name nevene?
>
> (*LGW*, vii, 2228-37)

We hear the poet's own voice in these lines, for, yielding to the God of Love in his dream, he has submitted to the command to tell the story of women celebrated in history for faithfulness in love. In the story of Philomela, the "flour of hire cuntre," Chaucer mourns over the ill-deserved fate of her "That nevere harm agilte." God made everything on this fair earth; but why did He see fit to allow such a one as the murderer Tereus to be born? The poet does not attempt to reconcile evil with God's justice, and the lines may be rhetorical. Yet he questions why this monster was brought into the world; and he does not dismiss the problem as beyond man's understanding, or point to the inscrutable will of God.

The same theme is pronounced in the *Franklin's Tale* with dramatic force but without reference to anything that was suggested in Boccaccio's version in the *Filocolo*, which Chaucer probably used. The lonely, loyal Dorigen, looking vainly for the ship which must bring Arveragus back to her, protests the dangers wantonly imposed on man. With resentment in her heart, she gazes fearfully down upon the rockbound shore.

> "But, Lord, thise grisly feendly rokkes blake,
> That semen rather a foul confusion
> Of werk than any fair creacion
> Of swich a parfit wys God and a stable,
> Why han ye wroght this werk unresonable?"
>
> (*FraT*, 868-72)

Dorigen is akin to the gentle Juliana of Norwich and would have understood the mystic's wistful observation, "I wondered why, by the great aforesaid wisdom of God, the beginning of sin was not letted, for then thought me that all should have been well."[117] Juliana found difficulty in reconciling the existence of sin in a world created by a wise God, just as Dorigen in the same perplexity pondered over a "parfit wys God" who permitted the existence of evil.

> "It dooth no good, to my wit, but anoyeth.
> Se ye nat, Lord, how mankynde it destroyeth?
> An hundred thousand bodyes of mankynde
> Han rokkes slayn, al be they nat in mynde,
> Which mankynde is so fair part of thy werk
> That thou it madest lyk to thyn owene merk."
>
> (*FraT*, 875-80)

If God so loved man that He made him in His own image, then why did He create evil forces that would destroy him? The inconsistency of such a God, whose ways she presumed to scan, perplexed Dorigen; like Palamon, she placed the burden in the more competent hands of the experts.

> "I woot wel clerkes wol seyn as hem leste,
> By argumentz, that al is for the beste,
> Though I ne kan the causes nat yknowe.
> But thilke God that made wynd to blowe
> As kepe my lord! this my conclusion.
> To clerkes lete I al disputison."
>
> (*FraT*, 885-90)

The patient, long-suffering Constance, the ideal Christian

[129]

lady, observes similarly how unjust fate can be, when even the life of a young and innocent child is unaccountably filled with pain:

"O litel child, allas! what is thy gilt,
That nevere wroghtest synne as yet, pardee?"

(*MLT*, 855-56)

Chaucer was disturbed by the problem of evil and when he came upon it gave voice to the same questions that were being raised by others. But unlike many Christian writers of his time, he never reproved those who rebelled against the divine will. Walsingham severely reproached Londoners who denied resurrection and put dogmas to the test of reason. Langland, still more sternly, took to task any who dared dispute with the Church, who presumed to ask for proof of things of the spirit. Wyclif denounced with bitter scorn the egotism of clerics who valued their own word above laws of Scripture. Gower assumed an attitude of pious superiority toward merchants who subjected the doctrine of immortality to the challenge of common sense. Guillaume le Maire, shocked by indifference to the Church, would punish all transgressions of those lost souls who speculated on, or ignored, articles of the faith. Deschamps harped against those who no longer believed in heaven or hell. Some blamed the devil, others pride. It is notable that Chaucer withheld judgment. Himself a man of simple faith, he stands out in contrast to other good men of his day by his understanding and sympathy, his failure to criticize the frailty of human nature in regard to faith. He was an observer, not an arbiter of mankind—perhaps because he was not certain of the fundamental doctrines of the faith he stoutly embraced.

In the last analysis, though keenly aware of the injustices in life and not deaf to the rationalists' criticism of orthodox doctrine, Chaucer placed his faith in Him who would "falsen no wight." The observation may be made that there are after all but few lines in Chaucer's works to reveal his critical judgment, his lack of gullibility, his practical attitude toward basic matters of religion. The wonder, however, is not that there are so few but that, in view of his profession of faith, there are any. Their importance here is to show how Chaucer's works were shaped, as Lowes has said, by his intercourse with men and by his reaction upon the interests, the happenings, the familiar matter of his day, in the light of which the lines discussed in this volume can be better understood.

Conclusion

IT IS IMPORTANT TO EVALUATE THE EVIDENCE OF SKEPTICISM
in the thirteenth and fourteenth centuries to give it its proper
proportion in the period when it became prominent. It should
not be supposed that skepticism sets the Middle Ages apart
from any other period. To trace the whole history of skepticism
would take us back to the ancients, to Lucian, Lucretius, Cicero,
Pliny, to Greeks and Romans and peoples of the civilized world
throughout history. For thinking men have always wondered
about creation and life and death, posed questions, and formu-
lated theories. Skepticism is not exceptional in a world that is
subject to the vicissitudes of time and fortune and human
conflict; in any century it is a world, therefore, that presents
constant problems to the mind of man. And man, yearning for
the realization of his vision of coherence and purpose in life
on earth, has tried eternally to solve these problems, to prove
the existence of God, to establish the presence of a divine law,
and above all to reconcile evil with a just providence. But it
was in the later Middle Ages that these problems came to be
discussed among laymen as well as clergy, among the folk as
well as scholars, that skepticism became an element in the
climate of medieval thought.

Limitation of the subject to the thirteenth and fourteenth
centuries has been arbitrarily imposed here because this was
the period of Chaucer and his immediate predecessors, and it is
the trend of thought within these generations of writers which
throws light on the thought and personality of Chaucer and
helps in an interpretation of his work.

His century was far from being an age of faith in the
strictest sense. Men were breaking with tradition, in religion
as elsewhere, and the doctrines which had been accepted without question were beginning to be subjected to critical and even,

Coulton has said, "hostile examination." It was a century described by Looten as the time when "la croyance chrétienne, si vivace à travers tout le haut moyen-âge et jusques et y compris le XIIIᵉ siècle, commençait à perdre quelque chose de sa vigueur et du puissant empire qu'elle exerçait sur les âmes occidentales."[1] Even the most faithful worshipers feared the Church was wrong—and so there was heresy and dissension; professed skeptics anxiously wondered if the Church might be right—so there were repentances and palinodes and recantations. Faithful Johns and doubting Thomases were neighbors—and Chaucer lived among them.

Chaucer lived among them, knew them, wrote about them. If some of them disputed about holy Scripture, applied rational standards to things of the spirit, laid "fautes vpon the fader," scoffed at threats of damnation, refused the Sacrament, professed atheism, Chaucer could not have been—and was not—deaf to their muttering. He talked about basic matters of faith himself—immortality and God's foresight and divine providence, subjects he went out of his way to introduce into works to which they were not always appropriate or of dramatic probability. If he was a man not out of accord with the Church—and of this there seems no reasonable doubt—was he not talking about things that were in the air, things he learned from his intercourse with men as well as from books? This seems all the more certain if he was sensitive to his environment, if he was one who, as Professor E. P. Kuhl has demonstrated in regard to certain of the *Canterbury Tales,* reflected public opinion.[2]

There is no contradiction in his profession of faith, on the one hand, and his questioning of the fundamental articles of Christianity, on the other, in the light of contemporary thought. For in every sense Geoffrey Chaucer was the mirror of his age—an age that looked back on an age of faith and looked forward to an age of reason.

Footnotes

[FULL BIBLIOGRAPHY ON BOOKS AND ARTICLES REFERRED TO IN FOOTNOTES WILL BE FOUND ON PAGES 168-175]

PREFACE

1. G. G. Coulton, *Five Centuries of Religion*, I, 188.
2. Etienne Gilson, *Reason and Revelation in the Middle Ages*, p. 60.
3. George Sarton, *Introduction to the History of Science*, III, Pt. 1, 13, 14.
4. Coulton, *The Medieval Scene*, pp. 111-12.
5. John Livingston Lowes, "The Dry Sea and the Carrenare," *MP*, III (1905), 45-46.

CHAPTER I

1. G. G. Coulton, *The Medieval Scene*, p. 111.
2. Coulton, *From St. Francis to Dante*, p. 313.
3. *Les Oeuvres de Guiot de Provins*, p. 38, lines 925-30:
   > Per foi lou seculeir clergié
   > voi je malement engignié:
   > il font lou siecle a mescroire.
   > Se font li clerc et li prevoire
   > et li chanoinne seculier;
   > sil font la gent desespereir.
4. *Ibid.*, p. 42, lines 1028-32:
   > mais jes voi si abandoneiz
   > en pechié et en covoitise,
   > qu'il ont desesperance mise
   > en la gent, qui molt tost mescroient.
   > Il meïsmes, je croi, mescroient.

5. Berthold of Regensburg, *Predigten*, I, 401, 402:
Sô ist nû daz dritte, daz den mânen dâ bezeichent, daz heizet ungeloube. Nû seht, wie manic tûsent menschen dâ mite verirret wirt, daz sie den hôhen unde den wâren sunnen niemer mêre gesehent! . . . Nû lât ez iuch erbarmen, daz sich got über iuch erbarme, daz sô manic mensche von unglouben verdampt wirt. Unde der mâne bezeichent ungelouben dâ von, daz der unglouben sô maniger leie ist. Die heiden habent sô vil unde sô maniger leie unglouben, daz des nieman an ein ende komen mac. . . . Unde dâ von bezeichent der mâne den unglouben, wan der mâne sô gar unstaete ist in sô maniger lûne. Er ist hiute junc und elter morgen; hiute nimet er abe, morgen nimet er zuo; nû kleine, nû grôz; nû gêt er hôhe an dem himel, morgen gêt er nider; nû hin, nû her, nû sus, nû sô. Daz selbe sint ungloubige liute.

6. Henry Adams, *Mont-Saint-Michel and Chartres*, pp. 252-53.

7. Gautier de Coincy, *Les Miracles de la Sainte Vierge*, "De la pucèle d'Arras à qui Nostre-Dame s'aparut," col. 273, lines 536-39:

> Qui honneur certes ne li porte,
> Et ses miracles bien ne croit,
> Il ne croit mie que Diex soit,
> Ne que Diex ait point de puissance.

8. *Ibid.*, "Le miracle Nostre Dame de Sardenay," col. 663, line 629:
Ne tient leur cuer ne foi ne créance.
Ibid., Prologue, col. 4-5, lines 68-72; col. 5, lines 87-88:

> Sovent m'avient que je sorri,
> De mautalent, d'ardeur et d'ire,
> Quant j'oi aucun buisnart dire:
> Que les miracles ne croit mie
> De madame Sainte Marie. . . .
> Cil qui ce dit n'est pas creanz
> Mes hérites et mécreanz.

9. *Ibid.*, "Du vilain qui à grant poine savoit la moitié de son Ave Maria," col. 625, lines 354-57, 361-65; col. 627, line 471:

> Vilain si fol sunt et si rade,
> Que bestial sunt comme bestes;

Ne veulent mais garder les festes,
Ne faire riens que prestres die. . . .
Envers Dieu sunt si endurci,
Que plus sunt dur de ce mur ci.
Ne doutent Dieu ne que mouton,
Ne ne donrroient un bouton
Des sainz commanz sainte Eglise. . . .
Peu ont créance et foi petite.

10. *Ibid.*, "De la fame qui recouvra son nez qu'elle avoit perdu,"
col. 174, lines 521-24; col. 175, lines 544-46:

Nes des lettrez sai-je de tieus,
Qui de venin sont si gletieus,
Que leur cuer point ne se délite
En la grace Saint Esperite. . . .
Simples genz font souvent douter,
Por ce qu'il gabent et qu'il rient
D'aucunes choses que cil dient.

11. *Ibid.*, "Le miracle Nostre Dame de Sardenay," col. 662, lines
574-76, 577, 598; col. 665, lines 704-06:

Mais il sunt maint larron prouvé/Qu'il nul miracles tant soit
granz/Ne prisent mie leur viez ganz . . . Créance et foiz en
aus défaut . . . Ne croient pas sainte escripture . . . Li mescréant qui pas ne croient, Que Diex tant de pooir eust/Que
de virge nestre peust.

12. Coulton, ed. *Social Life in Britain*, p. 197.

13. Etienne de Bourbon, *Anecdotes historiques, légendes et apologues*, pp. 195-96:

Item graviter et occulte temptat (dyabolus) de fide sub-
tiliter vel de spiritu blasphemie, de quo temptat frequenter,
cum alia ei deficiunt, pias mentes, et, ut eas in desperacio-
nem inducat, maxime simplices, vel ut a bono eas impediat.
Vidi aliquem pium et religiosum et probum clericum in
noviciatu suo temptatum, primo ultrum mundus aliquid
esset nisi sompnium aliquod, utrum ipse animam haberet, et
utrum eciam Deus esset.

14. Caesarius of Heisterbach, *Dialogus Miraculorum*, I, 209: dis.
iv, c. XL:

. . . quaedam sanctimonialis, femina provectae aetatis, et
magnae ut putabatur sanctitatis, a vitio tristitiae in tantum
est turbata, a spiritu blasphemiae, dubietatis et diffidentiae

adeo vexata, ut caderet in desperationem. De his quae ab infantia credidit et credere debuit, omnino dubitare coepit, nec ab aliquo induci potuit, ut divinis communicaret sacramentis. Quam cum interrogassent sorores, nec non et neptis eius carnalis, cur ita esset indurata? respondit: Ego sum de reprobis, de illis scilicet, qui damnandi sunt. Quadam die commotus Prior dixit ad illam: Soror, nisi resipiscas ab ista infidelitate, cum mortua fueris, in campo te faciam sepeliri.

15. See Chapter II, Part 2 below.

16. Charles V. Langlois, "Le Roman de Sidrac," p. 214.

17. In the prologue Sidrach explains that he wrote the book upon the request of Boctus, King of Bactriane (between India and Persia), whom he had converted to Christianity. After Boctus' death, the book had many adventures. It was said to have fallen into the hands of a Chaldean who would have burned it had he not been stopped by a divine intervention. It came successively into the possession of various kings and knights, finally turning up in Toledo, where it was translated from Greek into Latin. Another translation was made in Arabic, which reached Frederick II, who had it put back into Latin. Taken secretly from Frederick's chamberlain, to whom it had been entrusted, it was sent to Aubert of Antioch, whose clerk, Jean Pierre, carried it again to Toledo. And there it was for the first time translated into French.

18. "Sidrac," pp. 221-75.

19. *Ibid.*, p. 268:
"Cil qui se met parfondemont de savoir de la puissance Dieu est aussi fol comme cil qui voudroit la clarté du soleil enclorre en sa maison."

20. *Las Novas del heretje*, pp. 245, 251:
Ta fe e ton baptisme renegat e guerpit. . . . Tu non crezes c'om ni femna puesca ressucitar.

21. Robert de l'Omme, *Le Miroir de vie et de mort*, p. 515, lines 11-18:
> S'il muert, on li fait une lame,
> Com se tous jors i fust li ame.
> Cascuns, cascune sor chu beie
> Et dient tout: "Bien est ovree,"
> Et puis de la endroit s'en vont;

Pour l'arme autre orison ne font.
De l'arme quident mout de gens
Ke che ne soit el fors ke vens.

22. Caesarius, *op. cit.*, I, 33: dis. i, c. XXVII:
Cum venerit dies mortis meae, moriar, non illum potero bene
vivendo extendere, neque male vivendo praevenire.

23. J. A. MacCulloch, *Medieval Faith and Fable*, p. 200.

24. Coulton, *From St. Francis to Dante*, p. 317.

25. Caesarius, *op. cit.*, I, 207: dis. *iv, c.* XXXIX:
Male vivo, male valeo, et quare vel propter quem hic reclusa
sim, prorsus ignoro. . . . Quis scit, si Deus sit, si sint cum
illo angeli, animae, vel regnum coelorum? Quis ista vidit?
quis inde rediens visa nobis manifestavit? . . . Ego loquor
sicut mihi videtur. Nisi videam ista, non credam.

26. Coulton, *Social Life in Britain*, p. 218.

27. *Ibid.*, p. 224.

28. *Life in the Middle Ages*, tr. Coulton, I, 131.

29. Hélinandus, Moine de Froidmont, *Les Vers de la mort*, p. 32:
"Nos que chaille
De quel eure morz nos assaille?
Prendons or le bien qui nos vient!
Après, que puet valoir si vaille:
Morz est la fins de la bataille
Et ame et cors noient devient."

30. Rutebeuf, *La Chante-Pleure*, p. 96, lines 146-55; p. 97,
lines 158-59, 178-81:
. . . riens ne croit
Ne cuide pas qu'enfers ne que paradis soit,
Ne qu'il ait âme & cors por ce qui'il ne l'sentoit,
Ainz pensse li parfont que pechiez le deçoit.

Comment fet soi li bougres puet estre vérité,
Quar li clerc nos racontent en lor Divinité
Quant l'âme est espenie & el vient devant Dé,
Dient qu'ele est plus bele que li cors n'ait esté.

Je ne l' poroie croire, dist li bougres parfet,
Ce qu'Escripture dist ne que clergie retret. . . .

Si fete gent sont bien mescréant à véue:
Dient qu'âme de cors ne change ne ne mue. . . .

Or i a autres bougres si de Dieu mescréant
Qu'il ne cuident mie que Dieu soit si poissant,
Quant li mors est poris, qu'en autre tel semblant
Le puisse Diex refère comme il estoit devant.

31. Giraldus Cambrensis, *Gemma Ecclesiastica*, II, 285:
Sacerdos quidam nostris diebus ad alium, quem minus devote minusque reverenter divina celebrare corpusque Dominicum conficere noverat, zelo caritatis et correctionis accedens, cum ipsum in secreto super multis corripuisset, demum super hoc praecipue, quod tantum Dominici corporis et sanguinis sacramentum minus honeste conficeret, corripuit, et quoniam hostias nec puras quantum decebat, et candidas, nec etiam recentes vel idoneas, sed vetustate deformatas, ad hoc sacrificium assumeret. Cui miser ille in hunc modum respondit: "Quid est quod dicis? Dignus es odio cum religione tua. Putasne de hoc pane carnem vel hoc vino sanguinem fieri? Quinimmo putasne Deum Creatorem omnium de muliere carnem sumpsisse? Pati voluisse? Putasne mulierem sine coitu concepisse, vel post partum virginem fuisse? Item, putasne corpora nostra in pulverem redacta surrectura? Simultatoria sunt quae gerimus cuncta." . . . O quam multi similes isti inter nos hodie latent occulti!

32. Augustus Neander, *General History of the Christian Religion and Church*, IX, 9.

33. *Ibid.*, IX, 14.

34. Even his most ruthless critics do not accuse Boniface VIII of infidelity. Dante reveals his profanation of holy things and an unbecoming worldliness, but he does not place him among *unbelievers* in Hell. (*Purg.* XVI, 97-130.)

35. Philippe of Novara, *Les Quatre Ages de l'homme*, No. 147, pp. 81-82; No. 149, p. 83:
. . . li desesperé ou li mescreant dient que il n'i a autre siecle que cestui. . . .
. . . çaus qui dient qu'il n'est autre siecle que cestuy en quoy nous somes.

36. *Ibid.*, No. 140, p. 78:
Ce dient, et autres mescreanz i a, qui dient que touz jors a esté et est et sera cestui siecle, ne autres ne fu onques, ne est, ne ne sera.

37. Jean de Joinville, *Histoire de Saint Louis,* p. 197:

Le saint roy se esforça de tout son pooir, par ses paroles, de moy faire croire fermement en la loy crestienne que Dieu nous a donnee, aussi comme vous orrez ci après. Il disoit que nous devions croire si fermement les articles de la foy, que pour mort, ne pour meschief qui avenist au cors, que nous naiens nulle volenté daler encontre par parole ne par fait. Et disoit que lennemi est si soutilz, que quant les gens se meurent, il se travaille tant comme il peut, que il les puisse faire mourir en aucune doutance des poins de la foy.

38. *Ibid.*:

" . . . tu ne me tempteras ja a ce que je ne croie fermement touz les articles de la foy. . . . "

39. *Ibid.,* p. 230:

Jai veu en cest pais, puis que je revins doutremer, aucuns desloiaus crestiens qui tenoient la loy des Beduyns, et disoient que nulz ne pouoit morir qua son jour. . . .

40. Giraldus, *op. cit.,* II, 285:

"Caute nimirum antiqui, ut terrorem hominibus incuterent, et a temerariis ipsos ausibus refraenarent talia confinxerunt."

41. Berthold, *op. cit.,* I, 386:

Sô sprechent etelîche: 'der dâ ze helle gewont, der ist alse maere dâ alse anderswâ.' . . . Unde möhte der helle ieman gewont hân, sô möhte ouch er dâ wol gewont haben, wan er ist wol siben unde fünfzic hundert jâr dâ gewesen. Sô sprechent ouch etelîche, und ist mir ouch von gelêrten liuten für kumen, daz unser herre etelîchem ein hûs oder ein wesen in der helle gebe, daz im nihtes niht werre von keiner pîne.

42. The problem would long concern medieval people, opening up the whole question of salvation for the righteous heathen. See discussion in Chapter III, pp. 64-71, below.

43. *Aucassin et Nicolette,* p. 6:

"En paradis qu'ai je a faire? Je n'i quier entrer, mais que j'aie Nicolete ma tresdouce amie que j'aim tant; c'en paradis ne vont fors tex gens con je vous dirai. Il i vont ci viel prestre et cil viel clop et cil manke qui tote jor et tote nuit cropent devant ces autex et en ces viés creutes, et cil a ces viés capes ereses et a ces viés tatereles vestues, qui sont nu et decauc et estrumelé, qui moeurent de faim et de soi et de

froit et de mesaises; icil vont en paradis: aveuc ciax n'ai jou
que faire. Mais en infer voil jou aler, car en infer vont li
bel clerc, et li bel cevalier qui sont mort as tornois et as rices
gueres, et li buen sergant et li franc home: aveuc ciax voil
jou aler; et s'i vont les beles dames cortoises que eles ont deus
amis ou trois avoc leur barons, et s'i va li ors et li argens et
li vairs et li gris, et si i vont herpeor et jogleor et li roi del
siecle: avoc ciax voil jou aler, mais que j'aie Nicolete ma
tresdouce amie aveuc mi.

44. See below, pp. 44-47.

45. Caesarius, *op. cit.*, I, 304: dis. V, c. XXII.

46. Salimbene, *Cronica*, p. 69:
> . . . fuit quidam Gregorius Romanus, qui parvo tempore
> vixit, et mortuus est Mantue hereticus et maledictus. Quan-
> do enim in infirmitate sua portaverunt ei corpus Domini,
> noluit illud sumere, dicens, quod nichil credebat de tali fide.

47. Coulton, *From St. Francis to Dante*, p. 286.

48. Joinville, *op. cit.*, p. 197:
> Et je vous di, sire, dit li mestres, je nen puis mais si je pleure;
> car je cuide estre mescreant, psource que je ne puis mon cuer
> ahurter a ce que je croie ou sacrement de lautel, ainsi comme
> sainte esglise lenseigne.

49. Coulton, *The Plain Man's Religion*, p. 6.

50. *Choix des poésies originales des troubadours*, IV, 365:
> Ieu no mi vuelh de vos dezesperar. . . .
> S'ieu ai sai mal, et en yfern ardia,
> Segon ma fe, tortz e peccatz seria;
> Qu'ieu vos puesc be esser recastinans,
> Que per un ben ai de mal mil aitans.

51. *Les Lamentations de Matheolus*, p. 162, lines 77-78; p. 196,
lines 1301-06, 1309-11; p. 225, lines 2402-04, 2423-24; p.
226, lines 2428-30:
> Ha, Dieux! que je me doy bien plaindre
> De toy. . . .
> Car, comme tu soyes tenus
> A tous saulver, grans et menus,
> Pourquoy nous, pecheeurs, menaces
> Et nous condempnes et enlaces
> Sans fin a pardurable paine
> Pour une coulpe momentaine? . . .

> Pourquoy sommes nous telement
> Tourmentés pardurablement
> Pour pechié petit et legier? . . .
> Di pourquoy, par quelle raison,
> Pour le pechié d'Adam punie
> Est sa sequelle et sa lignie. . . .
> Chascun doit soustenir sa charge
> Selon sa coulpe estroite ou large. . . .
> Si semble estre contre droiture
> Que la lignie soit dampnable
> Du fait dont elle est non coulpable.

52. Philippe of Novara, *op. cit.*, No. 140, p. 78; No. 142, p. 79; No. 143, p. 79:

> . . . ce sont cil qui blasment et reprannent les oevres celestiaus et terrienes que li Peres createurs fist, et dient d'aucunes choses: "Ce n'est mie bien fait, et tele chose fust bone," et ainsic et ainsic. Entre les autres choses, dient: "Pourquoi fist Dieus home, por avoir poine et travail ou siecle et tribulacions, dès qu'il nest jusqu'à la mort? Et a la fin, se il le trueve en aucun meffait, si va en anfer; portant ne le deüst ja Dieus avoir fait." . . . Bien s'an devroient donc taire cil qui reprannent les oevres Dieu . . . commant osent il dire: "Por quoi fist Dieus home? et mialz vausist qu'il ne l'eüst pas fait!"

53. *Ibid.*, No. 147, p. 82:

> . . . les bons crestiens loiaus qui font les bones oevres et bien se contiennent vers Dieu et vers le siecle, ont sovant plus de persecucions et de maus en cest siecle que n'ont li mauvais et li delloial desesperé: cil en cui sont tuit li malice et toutes les mauveitiez, cil ont sovant plus assez des biens temporeus que li bon.

54. Joinville, *op. cit.*, XX, 196:

> Sire Dieu . . . pourquoy nous menaces tu? car es menaces que tu nous faiz, ce nest pour ton preu ne pour ton avantage; car se tu nous avoie touz perdus, si ne seroies tu ja plus poure, ne plus riche.

55. Wolfram von Eschenbach, *The Story of Parzival and the Graal*, p. 2.
56. *Ibid.*, p. 116.
57. *Ibid.*, p. 132.

58. *Ibid.*, p. 14.

59. *Ibid.*, p. 13.

60. *La Mort le Roi Artu*, p. 109: No. 103, lines 14-15:
"Ceste perte ne m'est pas avenue par la justise Damledieu, mes par l'orgueill Lancelot."

61. Jean Frappier, *Etude sur La Mort le Roi Artu*, p. 253.

62. *La Mort le Roi Artu*, p. 218: No. 190, lines 15-17:
"Ha! Dex, por quoi soufrez vos ce que ge voi, que li pires traïtres del monde a ocis un des plus preudomes del siecle?"

63. *Ibid.*, p. 219: No. 190, lines 22-23:
"Ha! Dex, por quoi me lessiez vos tant abessier de proesce terriene?"

64. *Ibid.*, p. 220: No. 191, line 14:
"Hé! Dex, por quoi soufrez vos ceste bataille?"

65. Frappier, *Etude*, p. 254.

66. *Gesta Romanorum*, ed. Hermann Oesterley.

67. *Ibid.*, p. 1.

68. Gaston Paris, *La Poésie du Moyen Age*, I, 155.

69. *Gesta Romanorum*, p. 397:
O domine, ecce homo iste culpam innocenti dedit et ipsum occidit; ex quo ergo permittatis talia fieri, ad mundum vadam et sicut ceteri vitam ducam.

70. *Ibid.*, p. 398:
. . . scias, quod nichil in terra fit sine causa.

71. *Ibid.*, pp. 478, 479:
Noli loqui adversus dominum iniquitatem, quia omnes vie ejus veritas, et judicia ejus equitas. Commenda memorie, quod sepius legisti: Judicia dei abissus multa. . . . . ne aliquid contra deum dicere presumas. Deus enim est justus judex et fortis et paciens, ideo non dicas: Quare fecit me et post hoc dimisit me cadere?

72. Of all those who have written on the subject, G. G. Coulton probably made the most intensive study of religious life in medieval countries, and he concluded: "The average of English church life was probably always above the general Continental average." (*Five Centuries of Religion*, II, 229.)

73. Coulton, *Five Centuries of Religion*, II, 172.

74. MacCulloch, *op. cit.*, p. 245.

CHAPTER 2

PART 1

1. Palmer A. Throop, *Criticism of the Crusade.*
2. Aziz Suryal Atiya, *The Crusade in the Later Middle Ages.*
3. *Ibid.,* p. 3.
4. James M. Ludlow, *The Age of the Crusades,* pp. 176-77.
5. William of Tyre, *Historia,* I, Lib. XVI, c. XXV, col. 668:
Quid est, benedicte Domine Jesu, quod populus iste, tibi tam devotus, pedum tuorum volens adorare vestigia, loca venerabilia, quae tua corporali consecrasti praesentia, deosculari cupiens, per manus eorum qui te oderunt, ruinam passus est? Vere judicia tua abyssus multa, et non est qui possit ad ea.
6. *Choix des poésies originales des troubadours,* IV, 42:
>   Mas la naus dels Sarrazis
>   No us membra ges cossi s banha;
>   Quar, si dins Acre s culhis,
>   Pro i agr' enquer Turcx fellos;
>   Folhs es qui us sec en mesclanha.
7. Ludlow, *op. cit.,* p. 360.
8. J. A. MacCulloch, *Medieval Faith and Fable,* p. 229.
9. *Histoire de la croisade contre les hérétiques albigeois,* p. 556, lines 8214-21; p. 570, lines 8442-45:
>   E lo coms de Montfort es tan fel e iratz
>   En auta votz escrida Dieus per que maziratz
>   Senhors so ditz lo coms cavalers esgardatz
>   Esta dezaventura ni com soi encantatz
>   Quez ara nom val glieiza ni saber de letratz
>   Ni nom ten pro lavesques ni nom val lo legatz
>   Ni nom te pro valensa ni nom val ma bontatz
>   Ni nom tenon pro armas ni sens ni larguetatz. . . .
>   El coms venc a so fraire quelh era plazentiers
>   E dechen a la terra e ditz motz aversers
>   Bels fraire ditz lo coms mi e mos companhers
>   Ha Dieus gitatz en ira ez amparals roters.
10. *Ibid.,* p. 572, lines 8461-66:
>   En auta votz escridan Dieus non est dreiturers
>   Car tu la mort del comte nil dampnatge sofers

> Ben es fols qui tampara ni es tos domengers
> Quel coms quera benignes e ben aventurers
> Es mortz ab una peira cum si fos aversers
> E mas los teus mezeiches deglazias e fers.

11. *Ibid.*, p. 590, lines 8744-49:

> E fas me meravilhas Dieus com pot cossentir
> La mort del sieu filh digne quel solia servir
> Mas pero per natura e segon quieu malbir
> Autre paire sirascra cant vei so filh morir
> Mas Dieus no fa semblansa quel sia greu nil tir
> ·Que can lor degra aucire fa nos dezenantir.

12. Guglielmo Figueira, in *Poesie provenzali*, II, 99:

> Roma, als Sarrazis   faitz vos pauc de dampnatge
> Mas Grecs e Latis   metetz e carnalatge.

13. Guillaume le Clerc de Normandie, *Le Besant de Dieu*, p. 74, lines 2563-64:

> Mult deust estre Rome mate
> De la perte de Damiate.

14. Matthew Paris, *Chronica Majora*, v, 108-09:

Coeperunt igitur multi, quos firma fides non roboraverat, tam desperatione et blasfemiis quam fame contabescere. Et fides, heu, heu, multorum coepit vacillare, dicentium ad invicem: "Utquid dereliquit nos Christus pro Quo et Cui hactenus militavimus? . . . Modo vero, quod omnibus gravius est, rex noster Christianissimus miraculose suscitatus a mortuis cum tota Franciae nobilitate ignominioso patet discrimini. Factus est nobis Dominus velut inimicus. Et Qui solet Dominus dici exercituum, nunc, proh dolor, a Suis hostibus tanquam multotiens superatus aspernatur. Quid nobis nostra devotio, religiosorum orationes, amicorum nostrorum prosunt elemosinae? Nunquid melior est lex Machometi lege Christi?" Et sic deliramenta verborum ex fide titubante resonabant, et dies Quadragesimales plus poenales quam poenitentiales deducebant.

15. Austorc d'Orlac, in *Mélanges Chabaneau*, pp. 82-83:

> Ai! Dieus! per qu'as facha tan gran maleza
> De nostre rey frances larc e cortes
> Quan as sufert qu'aital ant' aja preza?
> Qu'elh ponhava cum servir te pogues,
> > Quel cor el saber hi metia
> > En tu servir la nueg e l dia,

E cum pogues far e dir tom plazer:
Mal guizardo l'en as fag eschazer.

Ai! bella gens avinens e corteza,
Que oltra mar passetz tam bel arnes,
May nous veyrem tornar sai, de quem peza,
Don per lo mon s'en es grans dols empres.
    Maldicha si' Alexandria,
    E mal dicha tota clercia,
E maldig Turc, queus an fach remaner:
Mal o fetz Dieus quar lor en det poder.

Crestiantat vey del tot a mal meza,
Tan gran perda no cug qu'ancmais fezes,
Per qu'es razos qu' hom hueymais Dieu descreza,
E qu'azorem Bafomet lai on es,
    Tervagan e sa companhia,
    Pus Dieus vol e sancta Maria
Que nos siam vencut a non dever,
Els mescrezens fai honratz remaner.

16. Throop, *op. cit.*, p. 171.

17. Salimbene, *Cronica*, p. 445:
Irascebantur ergo Gallici, qui in Francia remanserant, tunc
temporis contra Christum, usque ádeo ut nomen Christi
super omnia nomina benedictum blasphemare presumerent.
Nam petentibus illis diebus fratribus Minoribus et Pre-
dicatoribus a Gallicis helemosinam pro nomine Christi,
stridebant dentibus super illos et illis videntibus, vocato
aliquo alio paupere, dabant ei denarios et dicebant: 'Accipe
pro nomine Machometti, qui potentior Christo est.'

18. Throop, "Criticism of Papal Crusade Policy in Old French
and Provençal," *Speculum*, XIII (1938), 380.

19. Ricaud Bonomel, in *Poesie provenzali*, II, 222-23, stanzas I,
III, IV:
        Ir' e dolors s'es e mon cor asseza
        Si qu'a per pauc no m'auci demanes
        O meta jos la crotz qu' avia preza
        A la onor d'Aquel qu'en Crotz fo mes;
            Car Crotz ni lei nom val ni guia
            Contrals fels Turcs cui Dieus maldia;

Anz es semblans, en so c'om pot vezer,
C'al dan de nos los vol Dieus mantener. . . .

Doncs, ben es fols qui a Turcs mou conteza,
Pois Ihesu Crist non lor contrasta ges;
Qu'il an vencut e venzon, de quem peza,
Francs e Tartres, Armenis e Perses;
    E nos venzon sai chascun dia,
    Car Dieus dorm qui veillar solia,
E Bafometz obra de son poder
E fai obrar lo Melicadefer.

No m'es semblan que per tan se recreza,
Anz a jurat e dit tot a pales
Que ja nuls hom que en Ihesu Crist creza
Non remandra, s'el pot, en est paes;
    Enans fara Bafomaria
    Del mostier de sancta Maria;
E, pus son Fils, qu'en degra dol aver
O vol nil plaz, ben deu a nos plazer.

20. *Austorc de Segret*, pp. 469-70, lines 5-8:
    Ni re no say, tan fort suy esbaytz,
    Si Dieus nos a o Diables marritz;
    Que Crestias e la ley vey perida,
    E Sarrazi an trobada guandida.

21. Throop, "Criticism of Papal Crusade Policy," *loc. cit.*, 380, n. 3.

22. *Les Derniers Troubadours de la Provence*, p. 44, lines 10-16; p. 45, lines 48, 57-60:
    —Tort n'aves, Dieus, e prendes autra via,
    Car vos donas poder a falsa jent,
    Qu'en fan quex jorn erguell e vilania,
    Qu'il non crezon ni fan ren que bon sia;
    E vos das lor sobras d'aur e d'argent
    Tant que n'estan crestian(s) recrezen(s),
    Car combatre nos pot hom cascun dia.

    E vos es leu quens gites a carnage.

    —Bel seinher Dieus, la gloria rial
    Pogras emplir s'esquiva ses lageza;

Pos conoises que tut(z) son deslial
Per que(l)s laisas reinhar en lur vileza?

23. Atiya, *op. cit.*, p. 114.
24. Throop, *Criticism of the Crusade*, p. 286.
25. *Ibid.*, p. 288.
26. *Ibid.*

PART 2

1. *Cambridge Medieval History*, v, 331.
2. Etienne Gilson, *La Philosophie au Moyen Age de Scot Erigène à G. d'Occam*, p. 124.
3. *Chartularium Universitatis Parisiensis*, I, 70:
   . . . nec libri Aristotelis de naturali philosophia nec commenta legantur Parisius publice vel secreto, et hoc sub pena excommunicationis inhibemus.
4. *Ibid.*, I, 78-79:
   Non legantur libri Aristotelis de methafisica et de naturali philosophia, nec summe de eisdem.
5. Henri Busson, *Les Sources et la développement du rationalisme dans la littérature française de la Renaissance* (1533-1601), p. 317. See Coulton, tr. *Life in the Middle Ages*, II, 65.
6. Matthew Paris, *Chronica Majora*, II, 476-77:
   Et post determinationem accesserunt quidam ipsius familiariores et ad discendum avidiores, postulantes a magistro, ut eo dictante quaestiones illas literis commendarent; dixerunt itaque indignum esse et jacturam irrestaurabilem, si memoria tantae scientiae deperiret. Quibus ipse elatus, et major sibi se, ait oculis sullevatis et temere solutus in cachinnum, "O Jesule, Jesule, quantum in hac quaestione confirmavi legem tuam et exaltavi; profecto si malignando et adversando vellem, fortioribus rationibus et argumentis scirem illam infirmare et deprimendo improbare."
7. Giraldus Cambrensis, *Gemma Ecclesiastica*, II, 149:
   "Deus omnipotens, superstitiosa Christianorum haec secta, et novella nimis haec adinventio quamdiu durabit!"
8. Caesarius of Heisterbach, *Dialogus Miraculorum*, I, 304: dis. v, c. XXII:
   Dicebant non aliter esse corpus Christi in pane altaris, quam

[149]

in alio pane et in qualibet re; sicque Deum locutum fuisse in Ovidio, sicut in Augustino.

9. *Ibid.*

10. *Chartularium Universitatis Parisiensis,* I, 449:
Statutum facultatis artium contra artistas tractantes quaestiones theologicas, et ne quis quaestiones, quae fidem attingunt simulque philosophiam, contra fidem determinare audeat.

11. Paraphrase by Antonius, archbishop of Florence, 1446-59, in *University Records and Life in the Middle Ages,* p. 73.

12. Charles Edward Mallet, *A History of the University of Oxford,* I, 61, n. 1.

13. *Ibid.,* I, 61.

14. Note that this is not Simon of Tournai referred to on p. 45.

15. *Chartularium Universitatis Parisiensis,* I, 48:
Disputatur publice contra sacras constitutiones de incomprehensibili deitate, de incarnatione verbi verbosa caro et sanguis irreverenter litigat. Individua Trinitas et in triviis secatur et discrepitur, ut tot jam sint errores quot doctores, tot scandala quot auditoria, tot blasphemie quot platee. . . . Hoc omnia, pater, correptionis apostolice manum desiderant.

16. *Ibid.,* I, 487:
Quod anima, que est forma hominis secundum quod homo, corrumpitur corrupto corpore. Quod anima post mortem separata non patitur ab igne corporeo. Quod humani actus non reguntur providentia Dei.

17. St. Bonaventure, "Collationes in Hexaemeron," XIX, 14, in Etienne Gilson, *La Philosophie de Saint Bonaventure,* p. 38:
In Ecclesia primitiva libros philosophiae comburebant.

18. *Ibid.,* XIX, 12, in Gilson, *op. cit.,* p. 37, n. 2:
Descendere autem ad philosophiam est maximum periculum. . . . Unde magistri cavere debent, ne nimis commendent et appretientur dicta philosophorum, ne hac occasione populus revertatur in Aegyptum, vel exemplo eorum dimittat aquas Siloe, in quibus est summa perfectio, et vadant ad aquas philosophorum, in quibus est aeterna deceptio.

19. Gilson, *La Philosophie au Moyen Age de Scot Erigène,* p. 120.

20. *Cambridge Medieval History,* V, 331.

21. *Ibid.*, v, 811.
22. *Historia Diplomatica Friderici Secundi,* VII, dxxviii.
23. Salimbene, *Cronica,* p. 351:
    Ut de homine, quem vivum includebat in vegete, donec ibi moreretur, volens per hoc demonstrare, quod anima totaliter deperiret.
24. *Albert's von Beham Conceptbuch,* p. 79:
    Ceterum non est mirum, si passim absque delectu injuste interficit homines, cum temporalem poenam non metuat, et minus aeternam, eo quod, sicut sui domestici asserunt, anima hominis perit cum corpore, juxta Sadduceorum haeresin, qui resurrectionem fore futuram et angelum vel spiritum existere non credebant. Verum apud tales omnis divinus cultus, leges Christi et evangelia vacua sunt et cassa.
25. *Historia Diplomatica,* v, 339-40:
    . . . insuper dilucida voce affirmare vel potius mentiri presumpsit quod omnes fatui sunt qui credunt nasci de Virgine Deum qui creavit naturam et omnia, potuisse. . . . et homo nihil debet aliud credere nisi quod potest vi et ratione nature probare. Hec et alia multa quibus verbis et factis catholicam fidem impugnavit et impugnat, suo loco et tempore sicut decet et expedit manifeste poterunt comprobari.
26. Salimbene, *op. cit.*, p. 351:
    Erat enim Epycurus, et ideo quicquid poterat invenire in divina scriptura per se et per sapientes suos, quod faceret ad ostendendum, quod non esset alia vita post mortem, totum inveniebat.
27. *Ibid.*, pp. 348-49:
    Nota, quod Fridericus quasi semper dilexit habere discordiam cum ecclesia et eam multipliciter impugnavit, que nutrierat eum, defenderat et exaltaverat. De fide Dei nichil habebat. Callidus homo fuit, versutus, avarus, luxuriosus, malitiosus, iracundus. Et valens homo fuit interdum, quando voluit bonitates et curialitates suas ostendere, solatiosus, iocundus, delitiosus, industrius; legere, scribere et cantare sciebat et cantilenas et cantiones invenire; pulcher homo et bene formatus, sed medie stature fuit. . . . Item multis linguis et variis loqui sciebat. . . . Si bene fuisset catholicus et dilexisset Deum et ecclesiam et animam suam, paucos habuisset in imperio pares in mundo.

28. *Ibid.*, p. 302:

Sed postquam mortuus est Fridericus, qui imperator iam fuit, et annus millesimus ducentesimus sexagesimus est elapsus, dimisi totaliter istam doctrinam et dispono non credere nisi que videro.

29. The book was successively attributed to twenty or more, first to Averroes and subsequently to Frederick II, Boccaccio, Machiavelli, Bruno, Spinoza, and Hobbes, among others.

30. Matthew Paris, *op. cit.*, III, 520-21:

Imponebatur enim ei, quod vacillans in fide catholica dixerit verba, ex quibus elici potuit non tantum fidei imbecillitas, quin immo haeresis et blasphemiae enormitas execranda. Fertur enim eum dixisse, licet non sit recitabile, tres praestigiatores sibi callide et versute, ut dominarentur in mundo, totius populi sibi contemporanei universitatem seduxisse, videlicet Moysen, Jesum, et Machometum; et de eucharistia, quaedam deliramenta protulisse. Absit, absit, aliquem virum discretum in tam furibundam blasphemiam os et linguam reserasse. Dictum etiam fuit ab aemulis suis, ipsum F (rethericum) imperatorem plus consensisse in legem Machometi, quam Jesu Christi. . . . Surrepsitque murmur in populum, quod avertat Dominus a tanto principe, Sarracenis a multo tempore ipsum fuisse confoederatum et amicum fuisse plus quam Christianorum.

31. George Sarton, *Introduction to the History of Science*, III, Pt. 1, 83-84.

32. Maurice de Wulf, *History of Mediaeval Philosophy*, p. 248.

33. Etienne Gilson, *La Philosophie au Moyen Age des origines patristiques à la fin du XIVe siècle*, p. 742.

34. Eugène de Beaurepaire, "Le Tombel de Chartrose," p. 237:

> Hélas comment la prophécie
> Voiez en noz temps acomplie,
> Quant plustost sunt les motz ois
> Du maleest Averrois
> Qui fu de toute sa puissance
> Anemi de nostre créance,
> Qui eslut vie et mort de beste;
> Quar nul ses oreilles ne preste
> A oir sarmons de la bible.

35. Petrarch, *Opera Omnia*, p. 913:
 . . . odi genus universum . . . vix mihi persuadebitur ab Arabia posse aliquid boni esse.

36. *Ibid.*, p. 734:
 Extremum queso ut cum primum perveneris quò suspiras, quod citò fore confido, contra canem illum rabidum Averroim, qui furore actus infando, contra dominum suum Christum, contraque catholicam fidem latrat, collectis undique blasphemiis eius, quod ut scis, iam coeperamus, sed me ingens semper, & nunc solito maior occupatio, nec minor temporis, quàm scientiae retraxit inopia, totis ingenii viribus ac neruis incumbens, rem â multis magnis viris impiè neglectam, opusculum unum scribas, & mihi illud inscribas, seu tunc vivus ero, seu interim abiero. . . .

37. *Ibid.*, p. 796:
 Fui nuper in hac nostra Bibliotheca, unus horum non quidem habitu religiosius, sed Christianum esse, ea demum religio summa est, unus autem horum dico, moderno more philosophantium quique nihil actum putant, nisi aliquid contra Christum, & coelestem Christi doctrinam latrant, cui cum nescio quid è sacris libris ingererem, ille spumans rabie, ac natura foeda ira, & contemptus supercilio frontem turpans. Tuos (inquit) & ecclesiae doctorculos tibi habe. Ego quem sequar habeo, & scio cui credidi. Verbo (inquam) Apostoli usus es, & fide utinam uti velis. Apostolus (inquit) ille tuus seminator verborum, & insanus fuit. Optimè, inquam, philosophe sequeris. . . . Ad haec ille nauseabundus risit. Et tu (inquit) esto Christianus bonus, ego horum omnium nihil credo. Et Paulus, & Augustinus tuus, hique omnes alii quos praedicas, loquacissimi homines fuêre, utinam tu Averroim pati posses, ut videres quanto ille tuis his nugatoribus maior sit.

38. *Ibid.*, p. 1055:
 Heu quàm dolendum, quod ingenium tale, fabellis inanibus irretitum fui. . . . Imò verò stultum te (inquit) si sic credis ut loqueris. Sed melius de te spero.

39. *Ibid.*:
 Quid de me autem speraret, nisi ut contemptor pietatis in silentio secum essem.

40. *Ibid.*, p. 1048:

Non modò mundi fabricam Platonis in Timeo, sed Mosaicam Genesim, fidemque Catholicam, totumque Christi dogma sanctissimum ac saluberrimum, & coelesti rore mellifluum, oppugnare non metuant, nisi humano magis, quàm divino supplicio terreantur, quo cessante, submotisque arbitris, oppugnant veritatem & pietatem, clanculum in angulis irridentes Christum, atque Aristotelem quem non intelligunt adorantes. . . .

41. Boccaccio, *The Decameron*, First Day, Story Three.
42. Gaston Paris, *La Poésie du Moyen Age*, ii, 146-47.
43. Frederick Tupper, *Types of Society in Medieval Literature*, p. 47.
44. *Encyclopaedia Britannica*, 11th ed., "Averroes."

CHAPTER 3

1. George Sarton, *Introduction to the History of Science*, iii, Pt. 1, 12.
2. In 1377.
3. Thomas Walsingham, *Historia Anglicana*, ii, 208:
Erant quippe tunc inter omnes fere nationes gentium elatissimi, arrogantissimi, et avarissimi, ac male creduli in Deum et traditiones avitas. . . . In tantumque excrevit eorum supercilium, ut auderent leges condere, quibus adventantes de circumjacentibus villis et provinciis, contra rationem omnem humanam, Deum, et justitiam, molestarent, gravarent, et fatigarent.
4. *Ibid.*, ii, 208, 12:
Praetereo eorum inhumanitatem, sileo rapacitatem, reticeo infidelitatem, transeo malignitatem, quam indisciplinate in adventantes populos exercuerunt.
Alii peccatis dominorum ascribebant causam malorum, qui in Deum erant fictae fidei; nam quidam illorum credebant, [ut] asseritur, nullum Deum esse, nihil esse Sacramentum altaris, nullam post mortem resurrectionem; sed, ut jumentum moritur, ita et hominem finire.
5. G. G. Coulton, *The Plain Man's Religion*, p. 8.
6. *Piers Plowman* survives in some sixty contemporary manuscripts. Note the long-continued interest the work has

sustained even up to our own time. The medieval master-piece has been edited and re-edited through the centuries, with a modernized version (Henry W. Wells, 1935) being reissued only recently.

7. Coulton, *Plain Man's Religion*, p. 8.

8. John C. L. Gieseler, *A Text-Book of Church History*, III, 196.

9. John Wyclif, *Trialogus*, p. 384:
   Nec dubium quin religiosi nostri privati tam infideliter ap-pretiantes signa sua sunt in isto capitulo, omnes enim tales sunt, 'inobedientes' legi evangelicae, cum plus appretiantur signa sua adultera quam fructum fidei, qui in lege evangelica edocetur.

10. *Ibid.*, pp. 352-53:
    . . . videtur esse ultra praesumptionem diaboli concedere participium meriti hypocritae sic viantis. . . . Quomodo ergo non dat haec haeresis viantibus occasionem publice delin-quendi? . . . Haec igitur haeresis fratrum supponitur esse causa, quare fides inter laicos sic vacillat.

11. *Chronicles of London*, pp. 67-68.

12. Guillaume le Maire, *Liber Guillelmi Majoris*, in *Mélanges historiques*, II, 477:
    Ex quo fit quod illis sacris diebus, in quibus precipue col-lendus [*sic*] esset Deus, colitur Diabolus, ecclesie remanent vacue, pretoria, taberne et ergasteria rixis, tumultibus, blas-phemiis, perjuriis resonant ibidemque fere omnium generum scelera perpetrantur. Ex quibus sequitur, quod lex Dei, articuli fidei et alia que ad religionem fidei christiane et salutem animarum pertinent, a fidelibus, quasi totaliter, ignorantur. Ex hoc Deus blasphematur, Diabolus reveretur, pereunt anime, fides catholica sauciatur; unde super tantis errore et abusu pernecessarium esset salubre remedium ad-hibere.

13. *Le Mireour du monde*, p. 51:
    Le plus grant orguel qui soit, c'est BOUGRERIE. N'est-ce mie grant orguel, quant un vilain ou une vielle qui ne seut onques sa patrenotre à droit, cuide plus savoir de divi-nité que tous les clers de Paris, et plus cuide valoir que tous les moynes de Cistiaux, et ne veut croirre que Dieu sache faire chose en terre que il ne puist entendre.

14. See above, Chapter I, pp. 13-14, 17-18.
15. See above, Chapter I, p. 22.
16. Juliana of Norwich, *XVI Revelations of Divine Love*, p. 223.
17. *Book of Margery Kempe*, p. 42 f.
18. Juliana of Norwich, *op. cit.*, p. 99.
19. *Ibid.*, p. 39.
20. *Ibid.*, p. 74.
21. *Ibid.*, p. 98.
22. Coulton, *The Medieval Scene*, p. 157.
23. R. W. Chambers, "Long Will, Dante, and the Righteous Heathen," *Essays and Studies*, IX, 50-69.
24. John Wyclif, *Tractatus de Ecclesia*, p. 11:
    . . . tantum est una, sic quod non multe ecclesie catholice.
    . . . extra sanctam ecclesiam catholicam non est salus vel remissio peccatorum.
25. Thomas Aquinas, *Summa Theologica*, Pt. III, p. 141: qu. 68, art. 1.
26. *Ibid.*, Pt. II, p. 45: qu. 2, art. 7.
27. Dante Alighieri, *The Divine Comedy*, p. 524, n. 1.
28. Francesco Sacchetti, *I Sermoni Evangelici*, p. 44:
    Puote uno, che viva e nascesse pagano o saracino, salvarsi, non avendo ancora battesimo? Rispondo che si, vivendo ragionevolmente e giustamente, facendo quello altrui che volesse che fusse fatto a lui. . . . Io ti rispondo, che la fede e la buona volontà fa salve ogni uomo.
29. *Merswins Neun-Felsen-Buch*, p. 63:
    . . . wo got findet einen also gar gerehthen guten heiden odder einen also gar gerehthen guten gudden, was dut denne got? ich wil dir sagen, got dar mag von sinner friggen minnen und von sinner grundelosen erbermede nut gelosen er kume in zu helfe; ich wil dir sagen, got der findet mannegen furborgen weg das er die gutwilligen gotmeinnenden menschen nut furlorn lose werden, si sint ioch an wellen enden si wellent in der witen welte. . . . wo dirre guter heiden odder dirre guter guden einer an sin ende kumet, so kumet imme got zu helfe und urlúhtet in mit cristoneme globen, das der criston globe imme also bekant wrt das er von allen sime hercen des dofes begerde wrt . . . so wil ich dir sagen was got denne dut, got der get und defet in in sime guten

begerden willen und in sime ellenden dode. Du solt wissen das dirre guter heiden und dirre guter guden fil ist in demme eewigen lebbende, die alle in sollicher wisen drin sint kumen.

30. Chambers, "Long Will, Dante, and the Righteous Heathen," *loc. cit.*, p. 54.

31. Juliana of Norwich, *op. cit.*, pp. 78-79.

32. *Ibid.*, p. 79.

33. *Ibid.*, pp. 25-26.

34. Coulton, *The Medieval Scene*, pp. 156-57.

35. *Ibid.*, p. 157.

36. *The Travels of Sir John Mandeville*, p. 200.

37. Coulton, *Five Centuries of Religion*, I, 450.

38. Thomas Aquinas, *Opera Omnia*, XIV, 462, 463:
Gregorius oravit pro Trajano, et eum ab inferno liberavit, ut Damascenus narrat in quodam sermone de mortuis; et ita videtur quod liberatus sit a societate reproborum orationibus Gregorii. . . . quamvis Trajanus esset in loco reproborum, non tamen erat simpliciter reprobatus; praedestinatum enim erat quod precibus Gregorii salvaretur.

39. *A Literary Middle English Reader*, p. 283, lines 6-9.

40. *Histoire Littéraire de la France*, XXIX, 549.

41. John Gower, *Mirour de l'omme*, p. 239, lines 21183-84:
N'ert pas de moy ce que je dis,
Mais a ce que l'en vait parlant.

42. *Ibid.*, p. 287, lines 25909-25920:
Ne sai pour quoy je precheroie
As tieux marchans del autre joye
Ou autrement de la dolour;
Car bien scievont, qui multiploie
En ceste vie de monoie
Il ad au meinz du corps l'onour:
Dont un me disoit l'autre jour,
Cil qui puet tenir la doulçour
De ceste vie et la desvoie,
A son avis ferroit folour,
Q'apres ce nuls sciet la verrour,
Queu part aler ne quelle voie.

43. Eustache Deschamps, *Oeuvres complètes*, VI, 109:
He! Dieu, quel temps et quel regne de monde
Court au jour d'ui par tout generalment,

Ou je ne voy vray cuer, pensée monde,
Pité, amour ne certain jugement,
Garder la loy, faire son sauvement,
Honourer Dieu ne doubter sa puissance!
Mais de touz maulx voy la perseverance
Es corps mortelz, en convoitant toudis
Fausses honeurs, dignitez et chevance,
Qu'a nul ne chaut d'Enfer ne Paradis.

44. *Ibid.*, VI, 219-20:

Parle qui veult, chastie qui sçara,
Blame les maulx, exauce les vertus,
Mette exemples chascuns telz qu'il pourra
De ceuls qui sont par pechiez confondus,
Les uns noiez et les autres pandus,
De l'ire Dieu, de tempest, de famine,
Mortalité, guerre, tourment, haine,
Des grans paines que fera Lucifer;
Tout ce monstrer ne vault par une espine:
L'en ne craint Dieu, Paradis ne Enfer.

45. Benvenuto da Imola, *Comentum super Dantis Aldigherij Comoediam*, I, 335:
. . . vir prudens et probus, ut dicetur statim; tamen imitator Epicuri non credebat esse alium mundum nisi istum; unde omnibus modis studebat excellere in ista vita brevi, quia non sperabat aliam meliorem.

46. Boccaccio describes Guido as an Epicurean, one of the best logicians in the world and an excellent natural philosopher: "Guido, being whiles engaged in abstract speculations, became much distraught from mankind; and for that he inclined somewhat to the opinion of the Epicureans, it was reported among the common folk that these his speculations consisted only in seeking if it might be discovered that God was not." (*Decameron*, VI, 9.)

47. "Of myself I come not: he, that waits yonder, leads me through this place; whom perhaps thy Guido held in disdain." (*Inf.*, X)

48. Benvenuto, *op. cit.*, I, 340:
Iste omnino tenuit sectam epicureorum, semper credens, et suadens aliis, quod anima simul moreretur cum corpore.

49. *Ibid.*, I, 357:
Fuit tamen epicureus ex gestis et verbis eius. . . .: Si anima est, ego perdidi ipsam millies pro ghibelinis.

50. *Ibid.*:
. . . nimis esset longum enarrare viros magnificos de secta epicureorum. . . . Ah quot sunt haeretici, qui simulanter videntur catholici timore vel poenae vel infamiae!

51. Sacchetti, *op. cit.*, p. 47:
Furono alcuna maniera di filosofi che diceano che in questa vita la natura producea a necessità ogni cosa, siccome fu ordinate dal principio del mondo; e non montava alcuna cosa orare o pregare, perocchè nel principio ogni cosa fu posta dove dovea rimanere.

52. See above, p. 63.

53. H. S. Bennett, *Chaucer and the Fifteenth Century*, p. 13.

54. Sacchetti, *op. cit.*, p. 97:
. . . che hanno tenuto con molte loro vane ragioni, che morto il corpo, morta l'anima. . . .

55. Walsingham, *op. cit.*, II, 282:
. . . videlicet non est Corpus Christi quod sacramentaliter tractatur in Ecclesia, sed res quaedam inanimata, pejor bufone vel aranea, quae sunt animalia animata.

56. *Le Mireour du monde*, p. 51:
Dont, pour ce qu'il ne peut entendre ne voir comment un homme entier puet estre en cele oublée que le prestre tient à l'autel, pour ce ne veut-il croirre que ce soit vraiment le cors Dieu.

57. Sacchetti, *op. cit.*, p. 97:
Credono gl' ignoranti, che credono i corpi nostri esser simili agli animali irrazionali, che in questa vita sono molti buoni che sempre avranno persecuzioni e fortune, e molti rei che sempre avranno bene.

58. Juliana, *op. cit.*, pp. 68, 72.

59. *Ibid.*, p. 121.

60. *Ibid.*, p. 217.

61. Jean Froissart, *The Chronicle of Froissart*, VI, 154.

62. Coulton, *Medieval Panorama*, p. 462.

63. MacCulloch, *op. cit.*, p. 229.

64. Mary Morton Wood, *The Spirit of Protest in Old French Literature*, p. 135.

CHAPTER 4

1. John Matthew Manly, *Some New Light on Chaucer*, p. 262.

2. Thomas R. Lounsbury, "The Learning of Chaucer," in *Studies in Chaucer*, II, 169-426.

3. Pauline Aiken, "Vincent of Beauvais and Dame Pertelote's Knowledge of Medicine," *Speculum*, x (1935), 281 ff.; "The Summoner's Malady," *Studies in Philology*, XXXIII (1936), 40 ff.; "Arcite's Illness and Vincent of Beauvais," *PMLA*, LI (1936), 361 ff.; "Vincent of Beauvais and Chaucer's Knowledge of Alchemy," *Studies in Philology*, XLI (1944), 371 ff.

4. Walter Clyde Curry, Chaucer and the Mediaeval Sciences, p. 218.

5. Bernard L. Jefferson, *Chaucer and the Consolation of Philosophy of Boethius*.

6. *Ibid.*, pp. 79-80.

7. John Livingston Lowes, "Chaucer and Dante's *Convivio*," *MP*, XIII (1915), 20

8. F. N. Robinson, ed. *The Complete Works of Geoffrey Chaucer*, p. 847.

9. *Ibid.*, p. 778, n. to line 1785.

10. Arthur Gilman, ed. *The Poetical Works of Geoffrey Chaucer*, I, xci.

11. Richard Morris, quoted by Robert Kilburn Root, *The Poetry of Chaucer*, p. 265.

12. Caroline F. E. Spurgeon, *Five Hundred Years of Chaucer Criticism*, I, 158.

13. George R. Stewart, "The Moral Chaucer," *University of California Publications in English*, I (1929), 126, 127.

14. *Ibid.*, p. 109.

15. Chaucer knew very well a whole series of satires against women: the *Roman de la Rose* of Jean de Meun, the *Miroir de Mariage* of Deschamps, the *Epistola Adversus Jovinianum* of St. Jerome, the *Liber Aureolus de Nuptiis* of Theophrastus, and the *Epistola Valerii ad Rufinum de non Ducenda Uxore* of Walter Map. (Robinson, *op. cit.*, p. 802.)

16. Adolphus Ward, *Chaucer*, p. 155.
17. John Edwin Wells, *A Manual of the Writings in Middle English* 1050-1400, p. 605; Root, *Poetry of Chaucer*, pp. 232-33.
18. Manly, *op. cit.*, pp. 244 ff.; Tyrwhitt, quoted by Walter W. Skeat, *The Complete Works of Geoffrey Chaucer*, III, 493-94.
19. Root, *op. cit.*, p. 25; Coulton, *Chaucer and His England*, p. 310.
20. Wells, *op. cit.*, pp. 604-05; H. Simon, *Chaucer a Wicliffite*, pp. 229, 292; Ezra Kempton Maxfield, "Chaucer and Religious Reform," *PMLA*, XXXIX (1924), 74.
21. Roger S. Loomis, "Was Chaucer a Laodicean?" *Essays and Studies in Honor of Carleton Brown*, pp. 129-33.
22. Simon, *op. cit.*, pp. 229-92.
23. See Caroline F. E. Spurgeon, *Five Hundred Years of Chaucer Criticism*, I, xix.
24. Looten, le Chanoine, *Chaucer, ses modèles, ses sources, sa religion*, p. 240.
25. *Ibid.*, p. 238.
26. John S. P. Tatlock, "Chaucer and Wyclif," *MP*, XIV (1916), 268.
27. Wells, *op. cit.*, p. 605.
28. Robinson, *op. cit.*, p. 15.
29. Bernhard ten Brink, *History of English Literature*, II, 57.
30. George R. Stewart, "The Moral Chaucer," *loc. cit.*, p. 101.
31. George Lyman Kittredge, *Chaucer and His Poetry*, p. 143; Howard R. Patch, "Troilus on Predestination," *JEGP*, XVII (1918), 410; Karl Young, "Chaucer's Renunciation of Love," *MLN*, XL (1925), 270-76; Root, ed. *The Book of Troilus and Criseyde by Geoffrey Chaucer*, xlviii-l; Tatlock, "The Epilog of Chaucer's *Troilus*," *MP*, XVIII (1921), 625-59; Curry, "Destiny in Chaucer's *Troilus*," *PMLA*, XLV (1930), 165-68, and "Arcite's Intellect," *JEGP*, XXIX (1930), 98; Looten, *op. cit.*, p. 242.
32. Robinson, *op. cit.*, p. 452.
33. Looten, *op. cit.*, p. 242.
34. Evidence points to a date between 1386 and 1390, since the piece is almost certainly addressed to Philip de la Vache, the events of whose life before 1390 would be more appro-

priate to the advice given here. See Robinson, *op. cit.*, pp. 976-77.

35. Root, *Poetry of Chaucer*, p. 30.
36. Tatlock, "Chaucer's Retractions," *PMLA*, xxviii (1913).
37. Aage Brusendorff, *The Chaucer Tradition*, p. 36.
38. *Ibid.*, p. 35:

Sic plures penitere se postea dicunt, quando mala sua et mala per eos inducta destruere non possunt; sicut Chawserus ante mortem suam sepe clamavit. 'Ve michi! Ve michi! quia revocare nec destruere jam potero illa que mala scripsi de malo et turpissimo amore hominum ad mulieres, et jam de homine in hominem continuabuntur. Velim! Nolim! Et sic plangens mortuus.

39. James L. Connolly, *John Gerson, Reformer and Mystic*, pp. 113, 115.
40. Lounsbury, *op. cit.*, ii, 459-536.
41. *Ibid.*, ii, 512, 514.
42. *Ibid.*, ii, 518.
43. *Ibid.*, ii, 520.
44. G. L. Kittredge, Review of *Studies in Chaucer*, ii by T. L. Lounsbury, in *The Nation*, liv (1892), 231-33.
45. Looten, *op. cit.*, pp. 233-35.
46. Lounsbury, *op. cit.*, ii, 509.
47. *Ibid.*
48. *Ibid.*, ii, 513.
49. John Bromyard, *Summa Predicantium*, Vol. i, "Fides," xxi-xxiii:

Qui ergo circa fidem modo predictorum infidelium errare voluerunt, scriptores sane intelligant, quibus innitentes necesse est credere que non videntur. Et hec est rationalis necessitas que nos compellere deberet, ut non visa crederemus que provenit tam ex divina iusticia quam ex humana consuetudine. . . .

Secundo ad idem necessitatem ex quotidiana hominum consuetudine in qua videmus quod cecus de via et sole et luna et aliis que non videt ductori credit videnti; patri etiam et matri vel ipsis mortuis aliis narrantibus quis noster fuerit pater vel mater credimus narranti; etiam de antiquis regibus vel legentibus cronicas vel romancias seu gesta de Karolo et Rolando et huiusmodi credimus que tamen nunquam vidimus. Ergo a fortiori ratione nostro ductori Christo clare videnti et sacris scripturis et legentibus et predicantibus de deo et salute animarum credere deberemus. Qui ergo de via celi et gaudiis bonorum et penis malorum non credit stultior est quocunque ceco qui puero credit. Et qui non credit que in scripturis leguntur quia ea non vidit stultior est omni ocioso auditori predictorum gestorum.

50. Lounsbury, *op. cit.*, II, 511-12.
51. Robinson, *op. cit.*, p. 784, n. to line 2805.
52. Tatlock, "Chaucer and Wyclif," *loc. cit.*, p. 266, n. 3.
53. Curry, "Arcite's Intellect," *loc. cit.*, p. 95.
54. Skeat, *op. cit.*, V, 92, note to line 2810.
55. Lounsbury, *op. cit.*, II, 514-15.
56. Tatlock, "Chaucer and Wyclif," *loc. cit.*, p. 266.
57. See above, pp. 64-71.
58. Lounsbury, *op. cit.*, II, 469.
59. Spurgeon, *op. cit.*, I, xix-xxi, 14-163.
60. Lounsbury, *op. cit.*, II, 470.
61. Sidney Hayes Cox, "Chaucer's Cheerful Cynicism," *MLN*, XXXVI (1921), 475-81.
62. Ward, *op. cit.*, pp. 149, 180.
63. Lounsbury, *op. cit.*, II, 473.
64. *Ibid.*, II, 519-20.
65. Looten, *op. cit.*, p. 226.
66. Coulton, *Five Centuries of Religion*, II, 379-413, 504-50, 553-647; *From St. Francis to Dante, passim.*
67. Lounsbury, *op. cit.*, II, 522.
68. Ten Brink declared that his "rationalistic reflections on religious problems have sometimes a skeptical tinge" (*History of English Literature*, II, 57). Wells believes his skeptical attitudes place him at the forefront of his age (*Manual*, p. 601). Coulton finds it "difficult to believe that the man . . . was a perfectly orthodox Catholic" (*Chaucer and His England*, p. 310). Root finds him "capable of questioning some of the tenets even of orthodox Christianity" (*Poetry of Chaucer*, p. 25).
69. Florence M. Grimm, *Astronomical Lore in Chaucer*, p. 54.
70. There is no evidence that medieval people made any clear distinction between *astrology* and *astronomy*, in the mod-

ern sense. Though Gower speaks of the two as separate branches of learning, he does not discredit the one in favor of the other. Wedel states that "Ever since the introduction of Arabian science, the distinction between astrology and astronomy had become hopelessly confused." (*The Mediaeval Attitude toward Astrology*, pp. 133-34.)

71. Thomas Aquinas, *Summa Theologica*, Pt. ii: qu. 95, art. 5.

72. *Ibid.*, Pt. i: qu. 115, art. 4.

73. Wedel, *op. cit.*, p. 124.

74. Eustache Deschamps, "L'Art de Dictier," *Oeuvres complètes*, vii, 268-69:

Astronomie est une science de la congnoissance des estoilles et des sept planettes erratiques et principales, c'est assavoir: *Mars, Mercurius, (Venus), Saturnus, Jupiter, Sol* et *Luna*; de leurs influences et disposicions selon leurs qualitez et conjunctions en divers signes et leurs opposicions, pour jugier des inclinacions naturelles des hommes selon leur nativité, et aussi des fertilitez ou sterilitez des terres et des fruis, des chauls et des froiz, des sentez et maladies des gens et des bestes; de sçavoir le compost du souleil et de la lune, de partir les ans et trouver les bisextes et leurs conjunctions des lunes pour ordonner leurs saingnies, et les temps de prandre medicine, et autres choses qui de ce se despendent.

75. Curry, *Chaucer and the Mediaeval Sciences*, p. 6.

76. *Ibid.*, p. 10 f.

77. Simon de Phares, *Recueil des plus celebres astrologues et quelques hommes doctes.*

78. Simon de Phares was first befriended in 1493 or 1495 by Charles VIII. Royal patronage soon roused jealousy at court and Simon's enemies finally brought him to trial for necromancy. His condemnation by the ecclesiastical tribunal was upheld by Parliament and his books and instruments were taken from him. It was forbidden that his works be bought or sold, and his professional career was ruined. He wrote the *Recueil des plus celebres astrologues et quelques hommes doctes* to justify himself in the eyes of the king, to whom he addressed the work. In his defense he describes astrology as a "pure science" and "one of the seven liberal arts," practiced by prophets, popes, cardinals, archbishops, emperors, kings, nobles, doctors, philosophers,

and clerks. Beginning with Adam and Old Testament sages he enumerates most of the Greek, Roman, and European writers up to his own time. It might have been a shock to Petrarch to find his name on the list!

79. *Ibid.*, pp. 127-28:
Galien, souverain medicin et astrologien, monstra bien en ce temps, en ses euvres, que nul n'est digne de soy nommer medicin, sinon qu'il soit bien instruit en la science des estoilles. . . . Entre autres bonnes choses, dit ou livre des *Jours cretiques*: "Tiengne et sache chacun medicin que, la Lune jointe avecques les estoilles fortunées, les maladies sont terminées à bien, et par la conjuction d'icelles aux estoilles contraires sont faiz et causés effectz opposites et mauvais, et pour ce doit le bon medicin premierement considerer en quel point est la Lune, c'est assavoir si elle est prime ou plaine, car lors croissent les humeurs et les moelles."

80. *Catalogue of Western Manuscripts in the Old Royal and King's Collections*, II, 23.

81. Kervyn de Lettenhove, ed. *Oeuvres de Froissart*, I, 456.

82. Wedel, *op. cit.*, pp. 142-53; Tatlock, *The Scene of the Franklin's Tale Visited*, pp. 22-37.

83. R. T. Gunther, *Chaucer on the Astrolabe*, p. v.

84. Tatlock, *Scene of the Franklin's Tale Visited*, pp. 17-37; Wedel, *op. cit.*, pp. 142-53.

85. Tatlock, *Scene of the Franklin's Tale Visited*, pp. 33-34.

86. H. G. Richardson, "Year Books and Plea Rolls as Sources of Historical Information," *Transactions*, V, 38, n. 1.

87. Pauline Aiken, "Vincent of Beauvais and Chaucer's Knowledge of Alchemy," *loc. cit.*, pp. 371 ff.

88. Manly, *op. cit.*, pp. 244 ff.

89. The only extant English translation of this work has affixed to the title: A Chronicle of Melusine in olde Englishe, compiled by Ihon of Arras, and dedicated to the Duke of Berry and Auuergne, and translated (as yt shoulde seem) out of Frenche into Englishe about 1500. (Jean d'Arras, *Melusine*, p. 1)

90. *Ibid.*, pp. 2-3.

91. *Ibid.*, p. 370.

92. Rupert Taylor, *The Political Prophecy in England*, p. 70.

93. *Ibid.*, p. 72.

94. Robinson, *op. cit.*, p. 823, n. to line 96.

95. Jean Froissart, *The Chronicle of Froissart*, IV, 203.

96. *Ibid.*, IV, 202.

97. Wedel, *op. cit.*, p. 142.

98. Walter W. Skeat, ed. *Piers the Plowman*, II, 155, note: a.11.158.

99. J. S. Brewer: "Chaucer [was] a Wickliffite, and therefore not favorable to the friars" (ed. *Monumenta Franciscana*, I, xl, n. l). John Foxe: "Chaucer seems to be a right Wicklevian" (*Acts and Monuments of the Church* [1583], II, 839; quoted by Lounsbury, *op. cit.*, II, 464). Gotthard Lechler: "There are several features of this portrait [of the Parson] which agree with the character of Wiclif, and not a single feature can be detected in it which does not suit him" (*John Wyclif and His English Precursors*, I, 299).

100. Tatlock, "Chaucer and Wyclif," *loc. cit.*, p. 267.

101. See above, pp. 48-50. See also Petrarch, *Epistolae* and *De Suiipsius et Multorum Ignorantia*, in *Opera Omnia* (Basil, 1581).

102. Coulton, *Five Centuries*, I, 433.

103. Loomis, "Was Chaucer a Laodicean?" *loc. cit.*, pp. 129 ff.

104. Stewart, "The Moral Chaucer," *loc. cit.*, p. 100.

105. Robinson, *op. cit.*, p. 768, n. to line 661.

106. Tatlock, "Chaucer and Wyclif," *loc. cit.*, p. 262.

107. See above, p. 17.

108. See above, p. 77.

109. Jean Froissart, *Le Joli Buisson de jonece*, in *Oeuvres complètes,* II, 24, lines 786-92:
> J'ai oï à parler souvent
> De la fontainne de Jouvent,
> Ossi de pieres invisibles;
> Mès che sont choses impossibles,
> Car onques je ne vi celi,
> Foy que doi à saint Marcelli,
> Qui desist: "J'ai droit là esté."

110. See above, p. 76.

111. Robinson, *op. cit.*, p. 943, n. to line 953.

112. Charles Trinkhaus, "The Problem of Free Will in the Renaissance and the Reformation," *JHI*, x (1949), 51-52.

113. See above, pp. 76-77.
114. Trinkhaus, "The Problem of Free Will," *loc. cit.*, p. 56.
115. See above, p. 77.
116. Stewart, "The Moral Chaucer," *loc. cit.*, pp. 105, 106.
117. See above, p. 79.

Conclusion

1. Looten, le Chanoine, *Chaucer, ses modèles, ses sources, sa religion*, p. 215.
2. E. P. Kuhl, "Chaucer and the Church," *MLN*, XL (1925), 334-36.

Bibliography

PRIMARY SOURCES

Albert's von Beham Conceptbuch, ed. Karl A. C. Höfler, Stuttgart, 1847.

Aucassin et Nicolette, ed. Mario Roques, Paris, 1936, 2ᵉ éd.

Austorc de Segret, ed. C. Fabre, *Annales du Midi,* XXII, 1910.

Benvenuto da Imola, *Comentum super Dantis Aldigherij Comoediam,* ed. J. P. Lacaita, Florence, 1887. 5 vols.

Berthold of Regensburg, *Predigten,* ed. Franz Pfeiffer, Vienna, 1862. 2 vols.

Le Besant de Dieu, ed. Ernst Martin, Halle, 1869.

Boccaccio, Giovanni, *The Decameron,* Modern Library, New York, n. d.

Bonaventura, St., *Hexaemeron.* See Etienne Gilson, *La Philosophie de Saint Bonaventure.*

Book of Margery Kempe, ed. S. B. Meech and Hope Allen, London, 1940. Early English Text Society.

Bromyard, John, *Summa Predicantium,* Basel, 1487.

Caesarius of Heisterbach, *Dialogus Miraculorum,* ed. Joseph Strange, Cologne, Bonne, and Brussels, 1851. 2 vols.

Chartularium Universitatis Parisiensis . . . cum authenticis chartis contulit ed. Henricus Denifle, auxiliante Aemilio Chatelain, Paris, 1889. 4 vols.

Chaucer, Geoffrey, *The Complete Works of Geoffrey Chaucer,* ed. F. N. Robinson, Cambridge, Mass., 1933. *The Complete Works of Geoffrey Chaucer,* ed. Walter W. Skeat, Oxford, 1894-97, 6 vols. *The Poetical Works of Geoffrey Chaucer,* ed. Arthur Gilman, Boston, 1880, 3 vols. *The Book of Troilus and Criseyde by Geoffrey Chaucer,* ed. Robert Kilburn Root, Princeton, N. J., 1920.

Choix des poésies originales des troubadours, ed. M. Raynouard, Paris, 1816-21. 6 vols.

Chronicles of London, ed. Charles L. Kingsford, Oxford, 1905.

Chronicon Angliae, ed. Edward Maunde Thompson, London, 1874. Rolls Series.

Dante Alighieri, *The Divine Comedy*, Carlyle-Wicksteed Translation, Modern Library, 1932.

—— *The Convivio of Dante Alighieri*, Dent edition, 1903.

Les Derniers Troubadours de la Provence, ed. Paul Meyer, Paris, 1871.

Deschamps, Eustache, *Oeuvres complètes*, pub. d'après le manuscrit de la Bibliothèque Nationale par le Marquis de Queux de Saint-Hilaire et Gaston Raynaud, Paris, 1878-1903. 11 vols.

Ethelred, St., *Beati Aelredi Abbatis Rievallensis Opera Omnia*, Vol. 195 in *Patrologiae Latinae*, ed. J. P. Migne, 1855.

Etienne de Bourbon, *Anecdotes historiques, légendes et apologues*, ed. A. Lecoy de la Marche, Paris, 1877.

Froissart, Jean, *The Chronicle of Froissart*, tr. Sir John Bourchier, Lord Berners, London, 1901-1903. 6 vols.

—— *Oeuvres*, ed. Aug. Scheler, Brussels, 1871. 3 vols.

—— *Oeuvres*, ed. Kervyn de Lettenhove, Brussels, 1867-1877. 25 vols. in 26.

Gautier de Coincy, *Les Miracles de la Sainte Vierge*, ed. M. l'Abbé Poquet, Paris, 1857.

Gesta Romanorum, ed. Hermann Oesterley, Berlin, 1872.

Giraldus Cambrensis, *Gemma Ecclesiastica*, ed. J. S. Brewer, London, 1862. 2 vols. Rolls Series.

Gower, John, *The Complete Works of John Gower*, ed. G. C. Macaulay, Oxford, 1899-1902. 4 vols.

Guiot de Provins, *Les Oeuvres de*, ed. John Orr, Manchester, 1915.

Hélinandus, *Les Vers de la mort*, ed. Fr. Wulff et Em. Walberg, Paris, 1905.

Histoire de la croisade contre les hérétiques albigeois, tr. M. C. Fauriel, Paris, 1837.

Historia Diplomatica Friderici Secundi, ed. J. L. A. Huillard-Bréholles, Paris, 1852-61. 7 vols. in 12.

Jean d'Arras, *Melusine*, ed. A. K. Donald, London, 1895. Early English Text Society.

Jean de Meun, *Romance of the Rose*, tr. Frederick Startridge Ellis, London, 1900.

Joinville, Jean de, *Histoire de Saint Louis*, Vol. xx in *Recueil des Historiens des Gaules et de la France*, Paris, 1840.

Juliana of Norwich, *XVI Revelations of Divine Love*, ed. George Tyrrell, St. Louis, Mo., 1920.

Langland, William, *The Vision of William concerning Piers the Plowman*, ed. Walter W. Skeat, Oxford, 1886. 2 vols.

Liber Guillelmi Majoris. See *Mélanges historiques*.

Life in the Middle Ages, tr. G. G. Coulton, New York and Cambridge, 1933. 4 vols. in 1.

A Literary Middle English Reader, ed. Albert Stanburrough Cook, Boston, 1915.

Matheolus, Les Lamentations de, ed. A.-G. Van Hamel, Paris, 1892.

Mélanges Chabaneau: Festschrift Camille Chabaneau, Erlangen, 1907.

Mélanges historiques, choix de documents, II, Paris, 1877.

Merswins Neun-Felsen-Buch, ed. Philipp Strauch, Halle, 1929.

Le Miroir de vie et de mort, ed. Arthur Langfors, in *Romania*, XLVII (1921).

Le Mireour du monde, ed. Félix Chavannes, Lausanne, 1845.

Monumenta Franciscana, ed. J. S. Brewer and Richard Howlett, London, 1858-82. 2 vols. Rolls Series.

La Mort le Roi Artu, ed. Jean Frappier, Paris, 1936.

Las Novas del heretje, in *Annuaire-Bulletin de la Société de l'Histoire de France*, XVI, 1879.

Paris, Matthew, *Chronica Majora*, ed. Henry Richards Luard, London, 1872-83. 7 vols. Rolls Series.

Piers the Plowman. See Langland.

Petrarch, *Opera Omnia*, Basel, 1581.

Philippe of Novara (de Navarre), *Les Quatre Ages de l'homme*, ed. Marcel de Fréville, Paris, 1888.

Poesie provenzali storiche relative all' Italia, ed. Vincenzo de Bartholomaeis, Rome, 1931. 2 vols.

Rutebeuf, *La Chante-Pleure*, Vol. III in *Oeuvres complètes*, ed. Achille Jubinal, nouv. éd., Paris, 1875.

Sacchetti, Francesco, *I Sermoni Evangelici*, Florence, 1857.

St. Erkenwald, ed. Sir Israel Gollancz, London, 1922.

Salimbene, *Cronica*, Vol. XXXII in *Monumenta Germaniae Historica*, ed. Oswald Holder Egger, Hanover and Leipzig, 1912.

Simon de Phares, *Recueil des plus celebres astrologues et quelques hommes doctes*, ed. Ernest Wickersheimer, Paris, 1929.

Sir Gawain and the Green Knight, tr. Theodore Howard Banks, New York, 1929.

Social Life in Britain from the Conquest to the Reformation, comp. G. G. Coulton, Cambridge, 1919.

Thomas Aquinas, St., *Opera Omnia*, Paris, 1871-80. 34 vols.

———— *Summa Theologica*, tr. Fathers of the English Dominican Province, London, 1911-25. 19 vols.

The Travels of Sir John Mandeville, ed. Ernest Rhys, Everyman's Library, New York, 1926.

University Records and Life in the Middle Ages, tr. Lynn Thorndike, New York, 1944.

Walsingham, Thomas, *Historia Anglicana*, ed. Henry Thomas Riley, London, 1863-64. 2 vols. Rolls Series.

William of Tyre, *Historia*, Vol. 201 in *Patrologiae Latinae*, ed. J. P. Migne, 1855.

Wolfram von Eschenbach, *The Story of Parzival and the Graal*, tr. Margaret Fitzgerald Richey, Oxford, 1935.

Wyclif, John, *Tractatus de Ecclesia*, ed. Johann Loserth, London, 1886.

———— *Trialogus*, ed. Gotthard Lechler, Oxford, 1869.

SECONDARY SOURCES

Adams, Henry, *Mont-Saint-Michel and Chartres*, Boston and New York, 1913.

Aiken, Pauline, "Arcite's Illness and Vincent of Beauvais," *PMLA*, LI (1936); "The Summoner's Malady," *Studies in Philology*, XXXIII (1936); "Vincent of Beauvais and Chaucer's Knowledge of Alchemy," *Studies in Philology*, XLI (1944); "Vincent of Beauvais and Dame Pertelote's Knowledge of Medicine," *Speculum*, X (1935).

Atiya, Aziz Suryal, *The Crusade in the Later Middle Ages*, London, 1938.

Beaurepaire, Eugène de, "Le Tombel de Chartrose et le Chant du Roussigneul," *Mémoires de la Société des Antiquaires de Normandie*, XX (Deux Série, 10).

Bennett, H. S., *Chaucer and the Fifteenth Century*, Oxford, 1947.

Brink, Bernhard ten, *History of English Literature*, New York, 1889-96. 2 vols. in 3.

Brusendorff, Aage, *The Chaucer Tradition*, London, 1925.

Busson, Henri, *Les Sources et le développement du rationalisme dans la littérature française de la Renaissance* (1533-1601), Paris, 1922.

Cambridge Medieval History, New York, 1911-36. 8 vols.

Catalogue of Western Manuscripts in the Old Royal and King's Collections in the British Museum, ed. Sir Geo. F. Warner and Julius P. Gilson, London, 1921. 4 vols.

Chambers, R. W., "Long Will, Dante, and the Righteous Heathen," *Essays and Studies by Members of the English Association*, IX, Oxford, 1924.

Connolly, James L., *John Gerson, Reformer and Mystic*, Louvain, 1928.

Coulton, G. G., *Chaucer and His England*, London, 1921, 3rd ed.

—— *Five Centuries of Religion*, Cambridge, 1923-36. 3 vols.

—— *From St. Francis to Dante*, London, 1907, 2nd ed.

—— *Medieval Panorama*, Cambridge and New York, 1938.

—— *The Medieval Scene*, Cambridge, 1930.

—— *The Plain Man's Religion in the Middle Ages*, No. 13 in *Medieval Studies*, London, 1916.

—— *Studies in Medieval Thought*, London, 1940.

—— *Ten Medieval Studies*, Cambridge, 1930.

Cox, Sidney Hayes, "Chaucer's Cheerful Cynicism," *MLN*, XXXVI (1921).

Curry, Walter Clyde, *Chaucer and the Mediaeval Sciences*, New York, 1926.

—— "Arcite's Intellect," *JEGP*, XXIX (1930).

—— "Destiny in Chaucer's *Troilus*," *PMLA*, XLV (1930).

Frappier, Jean, *Etude sur La Mort le Roi Artu*, Paris, 1936.

Gieseler, John C. L., *A Text-Book of Church History*, ed. Henry B. Smith, New York, 1857-63. 4 vols.

Gilson, Etienne, *La Philosophie au Moyen Age de Scot Erigène à G. Occam*, Paris, 1925.

—— *La Philosophie au Moyen Age des origines patristiques à la fin du XIVe siècle*, Paris, 1944, 2e éd. rev.

—— *La Philosophie de Saint Bonaventure*, Paris, 1924.

—— *Reason and Revelation in the Middle Ages*, New York, 1938.

Griffith, David Dudley, *A Bibliography of Chaucer*, 1908-1924, Seattle, Wash., 1926.

Grimm, Florence M., *Astronomical Lore in Chaucer*, University of Nebraska Studies in Language, Literature, and Criticism, No. 2, 1919.

Gunther, R. T., *Chaucer on the Astrolabe*, revised and abbreviated edition, printed for the author, 1931.

Histoire Littéraire de la France, XXIX, Paris, 1885.

Hort, Greta, *Piers Plowman and Contemporary Religious Thought*, London, 1938.

Jefferson, Bernard L., *Chaucer and the Consolation of Philosophy of Boethius*, Princeton, N. J., and London, 1917.

Jusserand, J. J., *English Wayfaring Life in the Middle Ages*, tr. Lucy Toulmin Smith, New York, 1920, 2nd ed.

Kington-Oliphant, T. L., *History of Frederick the Second, Emperor of the Romans*, Cambridge and London, 1862. 2 vols.

Kittredge, George Lyman, *Chaucer and His Poetry*, Cambridge, Mass., and Oxford, 1915.

―――― Review of *Studies in Chaucer*, II, by T. L. Lounsbury, in *The Nation*, LIV (1892).

Kuhl, E. P., "Chaucer and the Church," *MLN*, XL (1925).

Langlois, Charles V., "Le Roman de Sidrac," *La Connaissance de la nature et du monde*, Vol. III in *La Vie en France au Moyen Age*, Paris, 1927.

Lechler, Gotthard, *John Wiclif and His English Precursors*, tr. Peter Lorimer, London, 1878. 2 vols.

Lecky, W. E. H., *History of the Rise and Influence of the Spirit of Rationalism in Europe*, London, 1900. 2 vols.

Loomis, Roger S., "Was Chaucer a Laodicean?" *Essays and Studies in Honor of Carleton Brown*, New York, 1940.

Looten, le Chanoine, *Chaucer, ses modèles, ses sources, sa religion*, Lille, 1931.

Lounsbury, Thomas R., *Studies in Chaucer*, New York, 1892. 3 vols.

Lowes, John Livingston, "Chaucer and Dante's *Convivio*," *MP*, XIII (1915); "The Dry Sea and the Carrenare," *MP*, III (1905).

Ludlow, James M., *The Age of the Crusades*, New York 1910.

MacCulloch, J. A., *Medieval Faith and Fable*, London, 1932.

Mallet, Charles Edward, *A History of the University of Oxford*, London, 1924-27. 3 vols.

Mandonnet, Pierre, *Siger de Brabant et l'averroïsme latin au XIIIme siècle*, Louvain, 1911, 2e éd.

Manly, John Matthew, *Some New Light on Chaucer*, New York, 1926.

Maxfield, Ezra Kempton, "Chaucer and Religious Reform," *PMLA*, xxxix (1924).

Munk, Salomon, *Mélanges de philosophie juive et arabe*, Paris, 1927.

Neander, Augustus, *General History of the Christian Religion and Church*, tr. Joseph Torrey from 2nd ed., Edinburgh, 1847-55. 9 vols.

Owst, G. R., *Literature and Pulpit in Medieval England*, Cambridge, 1933.

Paris, Gaston, *La Poésie du Moyen Age*, Paris, 1913-22. 2 vols. (I: 7 éd., II: 5 éd.).

Patch, Howard R., "Troilus on Predestination," *JEGP*, xvii (1918).

Renan, Ernest, *Averroës et averroïsme*, Paris, 1866, 3e éd. rev.

Richardson, H. G., "Year Books and Plea Rolls as Sources of Historical Information," *Transactions of the Royal Historical Society*, London, 1922, 4th series, vol. 5.

Robertson, John M., *A Short History of Free Thought, Ancient and Modern*, New York, 1906, 2nd ed. 2 vols.

Root, Robert Kilburn, *The Poetry of Chaucer*, Boston and New York, 1934, rev. ed.

Sarton, George, *Introduction to the History of Science*, iii, Pts. 1 and 2, Baltimore, 1947-48.

Simon, H., *Chaucer a Wicliffite*, in *Essays on Chaucer*, London, 1868-94.

Spurgeon, Caroline F. E., *Five Hundred Years of Chaucer Criticism and Allusion 1357-1900*, Cambridge, Mass., 1925. 3 vols.

Stewart, George R., "The Moral Chaucer," *University of California Publications in English*, i (1929).

Tatlock, John S. P., "Chaucer and Wyclif," *MP*, xiv (1916).

—— "The Epilog of Chaucer's *Troilus*," *MP* xviii (1921).

—— *The Scene of the Franklin's Tale Visited*, London, 1914 for 1911.

Taylor, Rupert, *The Political Prophecy in England,* New York, 1911.

Throop, Palmer A., *Criticism of the Crusade, a Study of Public Opinion and Crusade Propaganda,* Amsterdam, 1940.

—————— "Criticism of Papal Crusade Policy in Old French and Provençal," *Speculum,* XIII (1938).

Trinkhaus, Charles, "The Problem of Free Will in the Renaissance and Reformation," *JHI,* x (1949).

Tupper, Frederick, *Types of Society in Medieval Literature,* New York, 1926.

Ward, Adolphus, *Chaucer,* English Men of Letters Series, London, 1923.

Wedel, Theodore Otto, *The Mediaeval Attitude toward Astrology,* New Haven and London, 1920.

Wells, John Edwin, *A Manual of the Writings in Middle English 1050-1400,* New Haven and London, 1916.

Wood, Mary Morton, *The Spirit of Protest in Old French Literature,* New York, 1917.

Workman, Herbert Brook, *John Wyclif, a Study of the Medieval Church,* Oxford, 1926. 2 vols.

Wulf, Maurice de, *History of Mediaeval Philosophy,* tr. P. Coffey, New York, 1909, 3d ed.

Young, Karl, "Chaucer's Renunciation of Love," *MLN,* XL (1925).

Index